This book is dedicated to the
faculty and staff of Bluefield State College.

CONTENTS

v

ABOUT THE AUTHOR

Mark Rowh is a widely published writer on career topics. He has contributed several other books in this VGM Career Books series, including *Opportunities in Electronics Careers* and *Opportunities in Fund-Raising Careers*.

Rowh also writes for major magazines such as *Consumers Digest, The Rotarian,* and *Consumer Goods Technology* and is a contributing editor for *OfficeSolutions* magazine. He is also the author of *Great Jobs for Chemistry Majors, Great Jobs for Political Science Majors, Slam Dunk Cover Letters,* and a number of other books.

He resides with his family in Virginia.

FOREWORD

The role of salesperson is one of the oldest occupational directions in human history. Even in ancient times, merchants made their living by providing goods people desired. Whether this meant selling food, spices, cloth, or other commodities, the act of selling became a basic part of everyday life thousands of years ago, a tradition that endures.

Today, sales professionals continue this long-standing practice in a wide range of areas. In some cases, this involves the marketing of traditional products such as agricultural commodities, clothing, or real estate. In others, though, recent technological developments have opened new vistas of opportunity. The sale of technical products or services covers a broad range of areas such as electrical equipment, electronic devices, computer software, communications equipment, and medical equipment and services, just to name a few.

Not only are thousands of technical products and services offered, but the complexity of many modern products requires special knowledge. This means that in addition to the traditional responsibilities of salespersons, those dealing with such products often find themselves in an instructional role. They may educate customers about equipment or software, help them choose from among alternative products, or provide advice in such areas as installation or repair.

With North America's growing population and the expansion of international trade and seemingly limitless advancements in technology, the need for skilled sales professionals will continue for the foreseeable future. This means that for men and women with the right interests, skills, and knowledge, career prospects may be extremely promising.

Are you a good communicator? Do you enjoy building relationships? Are you well organized? Do you have a flair for mastering information about technology? Can you be described as self-motivated? Do you like to set and exceed goals? If you possess these traits, one career path that might appeal to you is technical sales.

In *Opportunities in Technical Sales Careers,* Mark Rowh presents an overview of this diverse career area, including a look at the some of the jobs that can be found. If working in this area seems potentially appealing, you are invited to read further and check things out. Who knows? Perhaps a career in technical sales awaits you.

Ramon Avila, Ph.D.
George and Frances Ball Distinguished Professor of Marketing
Ball State University

ACKNOWLEDGMENTS

The author offers grateful thanks to the following for their cooperation in providing information for this book:

Dr. Ramon Avila, Ball State University
Manufacturers' Agents National Association
The Manufacturers' Representatives Educational Research
  Foundation
National Electrical Manufacturers Representatives Association
Linda Rowh
Sales Association of the Chemical Industry
U.S. Department of Labor

CHAPTER 1

THE NEED FOR TECHNICAL PRODUCTS AND SERVICES

At one time, a sales transaction was a simple matter. A peddler might sell a pot, for instance, or a farmer might buy an ax. In both instances, the product was something that warranted little explanation. The homemaker or other user of the pot knew just what to do with it. Similarly, the farmer understood how to use an ax to cut down trees, chop firewood, or perform other such work.

Today, simple transactions still take place, and some products require little special knowledge on the part of either the buyer or the seller. A pot is still a pot, and an ax is still an ax. But in the complex world of the twenty-first century, the same simplicity does not apply to all products and services. To the contrary, much of modern commerce is based on developments made possible by advancing science and technology. In an era where it seems impossible to keep up with the progress in a single field such as computing or genetics, few aspects of life seem as simple as they once were.

As a result, the practice of buying or selling many products or services requires considerations unheard of in earlier times. In many cases, customers can't simply choose a product based on common knowledge or their own experience.

For example, say a customer wants to buy a new scanner to be used in conjunction with a personal computer. The customer's questions may touch on complex matters, ranging from the computer's basic operating system to its capability for handling the software bundle provided as part of the purchase, not to mention the technical features of the scanner itself.

Or consider an instance in which a company intends to purchase a robotic device to be used on a manufacturing assembly line. The buyers may have a variety of questions about one company's product offerings in this area, including just how it compares with those provided by a competing equipment provider.

Who answers such questions? That is the role of technical sales professionals. These key personnel form a link between buyers of technical products or services and the companies manufacturing or selling them. The area of technical sales provides a variety of occupational possibilities. It is a field based on centuries-old business traditions. At the same time, careers in this area often reflect the latest technological advancements.

PRODUCT AREAS SERVED BY TECHNICAL SALES PROFESSIONALS

Typical product areas served by sales professionals that might be considered technical in nature include the following:

abrasives
acoustical material
adhesives and sealants
agricultural equipment and machinery
automation and robotics equipment
aviation products and equipment
biotechnology products and services
castings and forgings
chemicals and chemical manufacturing equipment
computer hardware and peripherals

computer networking services
computer software
controls and instrumentation
electrical components, equipment, and materials
electronic components, equipment, and materials
environmental products
fabrication machinery
Internet communication services
laboratory supplies and services
lighting products
lubricants and lubrication systems
manufacturing equipment
medical equipment and supplies
noise control products
office supplies and equipment
optical equipment and supplies
pharmaceuticals
Web development services
wireless communication equipment and services

These are just some of the many products and services in today's highly complex world that require specialized knowledge during the sales and marketing process. Appropriately trained sales professionals are routinely needed to serve potential customers while representing the companies offering such products.

RETAIL VERSUS WHOLESALE TRADE

Much of the business world can be divided into two major areas: retail and wholesale trade. Most salespersons focus on products offered through one of these two approaches to commerce.

Retail Trade

Salespersons in the retail business tend to focus on goods and services purchased by individual consumers. Establishments such as department stores, clothing stores, and supermarkets are typical retail enterprises.

The retail area is the largest single enterprise in which people work in a sales capacity. According to the U.S. Department of Labor, about 4.6 million people are employed as retail salespersons. Although the majority handle nontechnical products, a significant number sell products requiring an understanding of technical concepts.

For example, consider the large retail stores that specialize in computers and electronic products. If you walk into such a store in search of a new Web-camera for your computer, you will be greeted by sales staff trained to help you make a selection. Such employees represent the world of technical sales at its most fundamental level.

Similarly, customers who shop on-line or by telephone often have questions about the products they are considering. Many sales staff who handle such questions and help process orders also fall within the province of technical sales.

These types of jobs deal with a variety of different merchandise areas, but they share common responsibilities. Duties include both assisting customers in locating items and using persuasive techniques to interest them in making purchases. This may involve demonstrating products, describing their features, and comparing them with alternative choices. In the case of complex products such as computer peripherals or electronic equipment, this requires a basic understanding not only of how the equipment works, but of other factors such as ways in which equipment might best be used, compatibility with software or other devices, and the latest advances when compared with previous models.

Unlike many business-to-business sales positions, those in retail establishments often involve responsibilities such as handling cash, giving change, and dealing with returns or exchanges of merchandise. Other duties may include taking inventory or assisting in stocking products.

Another factor distinguishing retail sales from some other areas is the variety in working hours. Many positions involve working on weekends or during evening hours when stores are kept open for the convenience of customers. Part-time positions are very common. For those interested in exploring a sales career, they can be a good way to get started.

Educational requirements are usually modest, with a high school diploma the most frequent expectation. Of course, in more technical areas additional knowledge also is required, but it often may be gained through company training programs, additional class work, or self-directed reading and other study. Company training also may cover such areas as customer service, security and antitheft measures, and safety procedures.

Wholesale Sales

Wholesale companies focus primarily on the needs of organizations rather than individuals. They sell goods to retailers for resale to consumers, equipment and supplies to schools or government agencies, and other goods and commodities to businesses and nonprofit organizations.

In most cases, wholesale trade firms deal with goods in large quantities. Typically they purchase such goods from the manufacturers and then sell them in smaller quantities to their customers, who may be other wholesalers, retail businesses, government agencies, or institutional customers such as hospitals or nursing homes.

Wholesale trade firms come in several varieties. Wholesaler distributors, also known as merchant wholesalers, are the most common. They buy large volumes of goods from manufacturers and then resell them to other customers such as retailers, manufacturers or other wholesalers, or other customers.

Sales branch offices operate as local offices of manufacturers. They market products on behalf of their companies and coordinate their distribution.

Wholesale brokers, also known as agents, normally do not actually handle the products being sold. Instead, they coordinate the sale of products from one organization to another.

Sales personnel who work for wholesalers include many staff who deal with technical products. For example, a company specializing in computer chips might buy chips from several manufacturers and then sell them to companies that assemble computers or to retail firms that sell chips and other components to consumers. Sales professionals for such wholesale companies must be knowledgeable about the capabilities of their products and must take the necessary steps to represent their products to potential buyers.

Other sales staff might sell technical services rather than goods. This might consist of expert advice on technical matters or equipment installation and repair services, among other possibilities.

The overall wholesale trade area is huge. About 6.8 million people worked for wholesale trade establishments in 1998. A significant number—more than two million—worked in some type of sales or marketing capacity.

Typical sales roles include those of counter sales workers, who serve customers who come into an establishment to make a purchase; inside sales workers, who may take orders by telephone or on-line communication; and outside sales workers, also known as wholesale sales representatives, who go into the field and represent their employers' products. The latter include highly skilled personnel who make presentations to customers and potential customers, develop sales strategies, provide advice on the best use of products, and help customers solve problems through the use of their products.

THE TECHNICAL SLANT

When considering retail or wholesale trade or other elements of the world of commerce, an important consideration is the emergence of the technical angle involved in many sales transactions. Not every salesperson works in technical sales, but for those who do, some special capabilities may be needed. At the same time, such work may have much to offer in terms of both tangible and intangible rewards.

QUESTIONS TO ASK

In one sense, sales careers are nothing unusual. The role of the salesperson is one that almost everybody understands. It's not an obscure occupation, nor one that normally requires advanced education and skills such as those of a nuclear physicist or college professor. That's good news from the viewpoint of access, since this large, diverse career area is one to which almost anyone might aspire.

On the other hand, some sales careers can provide challenges that are far from mundane. With the increasing complexity of our technologically sophisticated world, sales professionals who deal with technical products and services often find their work genuinely stimulating. In the process, the potential for healthy earnings and other tangible benefits is strong.

For any one person, the appropriateness of a technical sales career depends not just on the possible rewards it offers, but also on individual interests and talents. In considering whether technical sales might be an area of potential interest to you, ask yourself questions such as these:

Do I have good communication skills?

Do I enjoy meeting new people?

Do I have an interest in advanced technologies such as computing or electronics?

Do I have a high energy level?

Do I work well independently?

Am I well organized?

Would I be comfortable persuading individuals or businesses to make purchases?

Do others consider me a hard worker?

Am I motivated by monetary goals?

Am I willing to obtain the necessary training to prepare for a job in technical sales?

Am I good at keeping records and following through on detail work?

If your answer to most or all of these questions is "yes," you may be well suited to a career in technical sales. If you are unsure about a number of them, think of steps you might take to evaluate your potential in this area (see Chapter 10 for more details) and take a look at the following chapters.

Chapter 2 covers the role of the technical sales professional. Chapter 3 looks at computer, electronic, and electrical equipment sales, and Chapter 4 covers pharmaceutical and chemical sales.

Chapter 5 reviews biological and biotechnology sales, while Chapter 6 covers other technical sales career areas.

Chapter 7 provides an overview of educational and training options, and Chapter 8 looks at professional associations.

Salaries and benefits in technical sales are discussed in Chapter 9, while Chapter 10 provides tips for getting started.

Once you've reviewed this material, perhaps you will want to take further steps in pursuing a career in technical sales. It can certainly provide some rewarding career area options!

CHAPTER 2

THE TECHNICAL SALES PROFESSIONAL

Too often, people are quick to criticize the role of the "middle man," referring to those people who stand between manufacturers and the end users of their products. But the truth is, men (and women) who serve in the "middle man" capacity render a valuable service. This is especially true for many technical sales professionals, because they possess specialized knowledge customers may lack. That hackneyed phrase, "I like to help people," may at first seem appropriate only for other professions such as social work or health care, but those in technical sales also may share a bit of this sentiment. With the increasing sophistication of products and services used in businesses and homes, their assistance can truly be helpful to consumers or business customers.

THE HUMAN TOUCH

As an example of the need for technical sales staff, consider Nora, a woman who recently started a home-based consulting business. She owns a computer, but has found that it lacks sufficient storage capacity for all of her data. In glancing through a catalog provided by a company specializing in computer-related products, she identifies a variety of options. Should she buy a computer with greater capacity? Or would it be smarter to install a bigger hard drive in her existing computer? Or perhaps she should consider adding a drive designed to hold super-floppies, or an external tape drive.

Answering such questions may fall within the province of a technical sales professional. If Nora describes her existing equipment and explains her needs, a knowledgeable sales pro can help her make a good choice.

This is not, contrary to some of the negative stereotypes attached to the sales profession, a matter of selling Nora the most expensive equipment available, or of talking her into buying something she doesn't really need. Rather, the sales process here means providing genuinely needed assistance. If the salesperson does a good job, Nora will be able to perform her own job more effectively. And at the same time, she will be a satisfied customer, likely to return to the same company when she has future equipment needs.

In the same way, sales professionals operating on a business-to-business level provide needed assistance. What happens when a business needs to obtain new call-management software for its telephone system? Or when a nursing home wants to update the monitoring equipment used to keep track of residents who need frequent medical attention? Or when a chemical company needs to find a replacement source for a large quantity of badly needed raw materials? In these and many other instances, technical sales professionals can play important roles. They may help customers make good choices, meet special demands when time is of the essence, help solve problems customers have experienced in previous communications, or provide other types of assistance.

In short, sales professionals in this area provide a badly needed human touch. Anyone can look at a list of available products, make a choice, and write a check or fill out an on-line order form. And with some types of sales transactions, that is sufficient. But when technologically advanced products or services are involved, that may not be good enough. Sometimes, much more is needed: the intelligence, experience, and willingness to help offered by appropriately trained human beings. That is the basic reason for the existence—at least from a business viewpoint—of the technical sales professional.

People who work in technical sales operate through several types of employment arrangements. Some work directly for manufacturers or wholesalers, selling products to businesses or organizations. Some are self-employed, in many cases representing more than one manufacturer. Some sell services rather than goods.

MANUFACTURERS' AND WHOLESALE REPRESENTATIVES

A major sales area involves serving manufacturers and wholesalers of technical products and services. In most cases, this means dealing with purchasing agents, retail buyers, and those with related responsibilities. Rather than dealing directly with consumers, they typically sell products and services to retailers, other manufacturers, wholesalers, nonprofit organizations, government agencies, and other businesses and organizations. In addition to marketing products and services, they provide advice to customers related to selecting and using them.

About 1.5 million men and women were employed as manufacturers' and wholesale representatives in 1998, according to the U.S. Department of Labor. This includes those working in nontechnical areas as well as the many who are employed in technical sales.

Job titles in this area vary. Typical position titles include Industrial Sales Worker, Manufacturer's Agent, Sales Engineer, and Sales Representative.

Some technical sales professionals are employed directly by companies to sell products or offer technical services, while others sell products offered by wholesalers. Some function as self-employed sales specialists who serve manufacturing firms on a contract basis.

Typical tasks performed by workers in this area include:

- meeting with buyers or prospective buyers
- traveling to meet with customers, attend trade shows, participate in sales meetings, or perform other functions
- providing sales literature, samples, or other materials to clients or prospective customers
- demonstrating how products can meet customer needs
- comparing products or services
- answering technical questions relating to terms of sale
- assisting in planning for or arranging training for customers
- completing sales reports
- identifying potential customers
- reading technical or sales journals and business publications
- tracking sales leads and analyzing data
- preparing reports

In some cases, sales pros also perform supervisory duties or other administrative tasks. These may include supervising other sales personnel or support staff, developing strategic plans, evaluating employee performance, managing budgets, and so forth.

INDEPENDENT AGENTS

A person working as an independent agent may sell products offered by several different manufacturers. This requires a high level of knowledge about the products being offered so that the best needs of the customer may be met.

The Wisconsin Association of Manufacturers' Agents (WAMA) notes that a manufacturer's agent is more correctly referred to as a manufacturer's representative. The role also may be referred to by other terms including "sales agent" or "sales representative." Shortened versions such as "sales rep" or simply "rep" also are common.

Several factors distinguish persons in this role. First, they are self-employed. Instead of serving as an employee of a manufacturer or retail firm, they represent two or more manufacturers in a sales capacity. Manufacturers also may be called "principals."

In this role, manufacturers' agents cover a specific territory. This may consist of a specified geographical area such as a multistate region, a single state or a smaller area. Or it might be defined by specific products, accounts, or a combination of several factors.

As pointed out by the WAMA, many manufacturers prefer this type of arrangement because it can provide them a national or international sales force at very low cost, since they do not pay salaries, fringe benefits, or travel costs of sales personnel. Instead, they only need provide assistance such as product training, sales literature, and sales leads, in addition, of course, to providing the products to be sold. Upon the sale of products or services, the manufacturer pays a commission to the manufacturer's representative.

For the manufacturer's agent or representative, this type of arrangement offers a number of advantages. Perhaps most important is the freedom to be one's own boss. Instead of working under the supervision of a sales manager or other supervisor, the manufacturer's rep sets his or her goals and objectives, controls daily work schedules, and exercises a great deal of discretion in when, where, and how to work.

Another advantage is solid income potential. For each sale, the manufacturer's representative earns a commission. This is a payment usually made as a percentage of the purchase price (for example, 5 percent, 15 percent, or 25 percent) of the item's cost. The more products sold, the higher the income earned. The rep also must pay for expenses out of this amount (which may include travel costs, secretarial support, salaries for subordinate salespersons, fringe benefits, and other costs), so actual take-home income is lessened substantially. But at the same time, the potential for earning an above-average income is excellent, and highly motivated sales professionals can do very well financially.

The Manufacturers' Agents National Association (MANA) defines manufacturers' agents as long-term independent marketing partners who maintain a steady presence within a given sales territory. In addition to selling products, they may provide extra services such as warehousing, consulting, or installation and maintenance services.

According to the MANA, the advantages of selling through professional multiline field sales companies can include the following:

1. predictable sales costs that increase or decrease with sales
2. lower average sales costs
3. increased sales, which promotes long-term relationships
4. immediate access to the market and enhanced experience and familiarity provided by an experienced sales team already in a given territory
5. free consulting services
6. reductions in training costs and turnover of sales personnel
7. experienced and aggressive sales force
8. accurate sales forecasting
9. broader sales context for manufacturer's products
10. marketing flexibility
11. efficiency provided by a systems approach to selling

12. strengthening of relationships
13. multifaceted, multiskilled sales teams
14. improved market intelligence
15. risk-free exploration of new market niches
16. vested interest in successful partnerships

These advantages not only apply to companies involved in such arrangements, but strengthen the position of individual sales professionals and support successful partnerships.

SERVICES SALES REPRESENTATIVES

At first thought, technical sales might call to mind specific types of equipment or other tangible products, such as computers or scientific instruments. But a significant demand also exists for technically based services. Examples include implementation of computer-based inventory control systems, development of Internet websites, assistance in selecting telecommunications systems, or design of computer networks, just to name a few.

Some sales professionals specialize in providing services instead of equipment or other tangible products. They might sell computer software, consulting services, or other services to companies, nonprofit organizations, government agencies, or individuals.

One company, for example, might specialize in developing accounting software and other programs used by businesses to maintain financial operations. Its key employees include salespersons who inform clients about software options, advantages of their firm's products, and the use of appropriate software, among other responsibilities.

Sales professionals who specialize in services fall into several categories. Inside sales representatives work primarily at their employer's place of business. Here they assist prospective customers or existing clients by providing information about the services offered by their company.

Inside sales representatives often are called "reps" for short. Much of their work is based on communication taking place through telephone conversations, although E-mail communications are becoming increasingly common. They also may send fax messages, assemble packets of information, prepare sales proposals, or perform related tasks.

In some cases, inside sales representatives take a proactive approach, contacting potential customers and offering them the services available from their companies. In other instances, they wait to be contacted by customers, responding to calls and other inquiries.

Another category is that of outside sales representatives. Workers fulfilling this role call on prospective customers at locations such as offices, factories, or homes, although the latter is less common for those in technical fields than in general sales. A third category, that of telemarketing sales representatives, is also less common in technical sales than in areas such as communications and financial services.

TYPICAL POSITIONS

Regardless of the mode of operation, almost all sales professionals share certain common responsibilities. They must develop a high level of knowledge about the products or services offered, and they must possess or acquire the communication, organization, and human relations skills needed to interact successfully with customers and fellow employees.

Often, an individual holding a technical sales position has been trained in engineering or a scientific field and has elected to use this background in sales rather than in another role.

All those who work in technical sales, however, do not boast engineering degrees or scientific backgrounds. Quite often, educational preparation or employment experience in business leads to such work. This might involve training in sales or marketing, or it might be based on more general skills in business administration.

In cases where a sales professional has not developed a highly technical background, he or she may team up with one or more technical experts. In such an arrangement, a technical specialist may participate in a sales presentation or provide follow-up service after a sale, while the sales representative conducts the bulk of activities directly related to the sales process.

Once they are placed in sales positions, people who work in this field assume specific job roles based on the responsibilities assigned to particular types of positions. Here are overviews of some representative positions.

Sales Order Administrator

Typically, this position would be responsible for coordinating orders placed by customers. This might involve tasks such as answering the phone or handling on-line orders, receiving and documenting customer purchase orders, and routing customer purchase orders to the appropriate departments or individuals. Other tasks might include preparing packing lists, communicating with customers when follow-up is needed, preparing invoices, preparing reports, and maintaining files and other documentation.

Demonstration Specialist

Another sales-related position is that of demonstration specialist or demonstration support specialist. This job involves making sales presentations or assisting others in preparing and presenting information. Typical duties include creating presentations; writing business proposals; using presentation software to prepare graphs, charts, and other illustrations; and utilizing high-tech equipment to present information. A major role is speaking before groups of various sizes to provide overviews of available products and answer questions from potential customers.

Sales Engineer

One of the most challenging positions in this area is that of sales engineer. Sales engineers use substantial technical knowledge to inform potential customers about the features of products, help them in making selections, and provide assistance in using them. The latter might entail equipment or software installation, training in equipment use, or other steps in how to assist customers make optimum use of products.

According to the University of Florida, sales engineers strive to bridge the communication gap between those who manufacture technological products and consumers who purchase them. They serve in an intermediary role between manufacturers and engineers and nontechnical professionals. A major role of sales engineers is to supply product information and identify customer needs. To fulfill this role, they must thoroughly understand a given product's design and performance characteristics as well as hold a solid grasp of its function. Sales engineers also must understand the products offered by competitors and be able to communicate this information to customers and potential customers. Their job includes tasks related to selecting, buying, installing, and maintaining technical products.

Sales Manager

Sales managers perform a variety of tasks. To perform their jobs, they must be knowledgeable about topics such as buyer behavior, market segmentation, methods of assessing marketing efforts, sales forecasting, and organizational theory.

Major job responsibilities of sales managers include recruiting, selecting, and training sales staff. They also may be responsible for motivating employees, providing a broad range of management oversight, and evaluating sales activities as well as the performance of individual employees.

Other roles of sales managers include organizing and coordinating sales territories, conducting financial planning, developing sales forecasts, evaluating market segments, and developing competitive marketing strategies.

Sales management can provide an attractive career path. According to the U.S. Department of Labor, roles as marketing, sales, or advertising managers rank among the top careers for the twenty-first century, with growth rates expected to be extremely high.

Other typical job titles in technical sales include:

Account Executive
Account Manager
Alliance Manager
Business Development Manager
Channel Manager
Customer Relationship Manager
Director of Marketing
Director of Sales
Inside Sales Representative
International Account Executive
Marketing Manager
Marketing Representative
National Alliance Manager
National Channel Manager
Regional Sales Manager
Sales Associate
Sales Manager
Sales Representative
Vice President of Sales

SKILLS REQUIRED

Not everyone can be an effective technical sales professional. Those who are shy or introverted may find they cannot function well in communicating with others and in acting persuasively to meet sales goals. Those who lack a flair for mastering technical concepts may find they are not up to the task of explaining the features of technical products or services, or of answering questions posed by customers or potential customers. Those who lack an aggressive or ambitious style, who are not self-directed, or who are not goal oriented, may lack the level of initiative needed to succeed in a sales career.

Most successful sales personnel exhibit certain basic traits or skills. For example, they possess or develop the ability to establish rapport with customers. They also learn techniques for helping customers focus on their needs or desires, overcoming customers' resistance to making a purchase, and finishing sales transactions.

Those who are most effective tend to take a flexible approach to the sales process. When necessary, they are able to adapt their style to communicate in the most effective manner with any given prospective customer. They also balance their own desire to make a sale with the natural reticence some customers exhibit, avoiding a high-pressure style, which tends to alienate many customers. This includes learning to "read" customers and then following up appropriately from the initial contact to the conclusion of a sale.

Pharmaceutical manufacturer Lilly, for example, asks that its salespeople have traits including the following:

- be achievement-focused
- have high self-motivation
- possess good problem-solving skills
- have excellent communication/interpersonal skills

- have good negotiating skills
- possess project selling skills
- possess a return-on-investment mentality
- be a team player
- have excellent organizational skills

Ability to Build Relationships

A key to successful sales, insiders will tell you, is the ability to build and maintain relationships. Winners in the sales game don't just make one sale to a customer and then move on to the next. Although the need to identify new customers is a continuing one, of great importance is the ability to make repeat sales to existing customers or clients. For this to occur, a solid working relationship must be established.

Why would a customer return to a company that has previously provided products or services? Of course, the quality of a product is paramount, as is cost. But buyers also respond to previous experience. If they have been well treated, they are more likely to offer repeat business. What constitutes good treatment varies from one customer to another, but in general it involves factors such as promptness in responding to phone calls or other messages, reliability in meeting deadlines or schedules, clear communications, a lack of frequent mistakes or misunderstandings, mutual respect, and a belief that high ethical standards are consistently being observed.

As salespeople interact with customers, they gain opportunities for continuing a positive business relationship. This can be beneficial to both parties. For the customer, it is helpful to be able to deal with a reliable salesperson who is a "known quantity." Instead of starting from scratch whenever a new purchase must be made, the customer can save time and effort by dealing with a sales contact he or she knows and trusts. At the same time, the sales professional benefits from making new sales while continuing the mutually positive relationship.

In an entirely different way, building relationships provides sales professionals with some important intrinsic rewards. Making sales means making money, but life—and work—is more than simply reaping financial rewards. Most salespeople take pleasure in other aspects of the job: helping customers, exchanging pleasant conversation, and sometimes getting to know customers as people and not just sales prospects. In fact, most of those who are successful in the sales arena will readily describe themselves as "people persons," meaning they enjoy interacting with others and tend to have a natural affinity for personal communication. For such people, a sales career can combine occupational goals with personal interests. On a daily basis, this translates to working in an area where the tasks involved can be enjoyable as well as productive.

Computer Skills

An increasingly important skill in the world of sales is the use of computers. This includes both desktop computers and portable computers or related devices such as personal digital assistants (PDAs).

Many sales personnel make extensive use of computers, especially laptop or notebook models, which are handy for their portability. They employ them to write memos, letters, and reports using word processing software; prepare and give sales presentations; manage databases and track customers; send and receive E-mail; and perform other activities involved in communicating with customers, peers, and superiors as well as maintaining sale-related data.

ADVANTAGES OF A TECHNICAL SALES CAREER

Some of the responsibilities related to sales positions may be seen as either advantages or disadvantages, depending on one's personal outlook. For example, many sales jobs require moderate to extensive travel. This may be seen as inconvenient or tiresome to some people, but exciting and interesting to others.

Similarly, some people may be reluctant to enter into the persuasive mode sometimes required of successful sales professionals. Others may find this challenging and enjoyable.

For most people interested in this area, some common advantages are generally recognized. These range from the ability to earn good or excellent incomes to less tangible rewards such as the mental challenge involved in working with complex technical concepts.

The Profit Incentive

A major incentive for employment is pay. This may sound too simple even to state, but careers are a complicated business, and sometimes the matter of income potential is overshadowed by other considerations. How many times have you heard someone say that being happy in your work is more important than how much money you make?

Certainly there is great truth in this statement, and anyone who pursues a career just for financial rewards is probably destined for unhappiness. But if you enjoy your work and earn enough income to meet your desired lifestyle needs, you can have the best of both worlds.

This is the potential offered by sales careers, both in technical and nontechnical areas. Assuming that you enjoy the work involved, a sales career offers the added advantage of solid income potential.

One plus with this area is that the harder you are willing to work, the more money it is possible to earn, at least in general. Certainly there are no guarantees, and a sales pro can put in many hours of work only to find that a customer has chosen a different supplier or has decided not to make a purchase after all. But on an overall basis, the potential exists to earn greater rewards commensurate with one's effort.

In other words, the more you sell, the more you make. Most sales positions involve some combination of salary, commissions, and bonuses. With commissions, each sale results in a payment to the salesperson based on an agreed-upon formula. With bonuses, lump sums are awarded for reaching a specified sales volume or meeting other criteria. Even with salaries alone, pay raises or promotions may be in order for successful performance.

The bottom line is that the best sales professionals in any field can earn impressive incomes. Certainly there is risk involved, for if sales volume is low, just the opposite can occur. But for those willing to work hard and take the steps necessary for success, a sales career can be a lucrative one.

If nothing else, the pay-on-performance nature of sales work at least holds the potential for financial rewards to be consistent with the effort put forth. Compare this to some other types of jobs, such as a wage-based factory job in which wages are determined by a union contract. In such cases, one worker might do everything possible to do a good job during her or his shift, while another may do just the minimum. Both are paid the same hourly wage, with no financial incentive for the harder-working employee. This is definitely not the case where employees may earn commissions, bonuses, or other incentives.

Challenging Roles

Another advantage of a technical sales career is that it can provide more intellectual stimulation than many other sales areas. Because of the continuing advancement of technology, those working in all related areas, including sales and marketing, must constantly master new information. Anyone whose job involves selling computers or software, for instance, must stay aware of very rapid changes in capabilities, features, and other details to be effective. This might require reading journals or other written material, attending classes or seminars, running demonstrations, personally working with new equipment, or taking other steps to master new developments.

Through such measures and through the process of communicating with various business professionals, clients, and others, sales pros find themselves on the cutting edge of new knowledge. The results are frequently stimulating in terms of the sheer enjoyment of mastering interesting concepts.

Potential for Advancement

Another attractive feature of a technical sales career is the potential for career advancement. This may involve any number of approaches.

One way to advance in this field is to remain in a sales track but to earn higher salaries and other perquisites as one's success level increases. In many cases, experienced sales professionals find their job status improving substantially as they gain experience. This may consist of steps such as being assigned to more lucrative accounts, earning a more desirable sales territory from a geographical viewpoint, earning cash bonuses, or winning awards and prizes such as vacations.

Another career path is to move into a sales management position. It is not uncommon for successful sales professionals to earn promotions in which their new role includes significant managerial responsibilities. These may entail hiring and supervising other salespersons, setting sales goals, coordinating the preparation of sales reports, and dealing with other administrative tasks. In some cases, sales managers combine the work of selling with a supervisory role; in others, they are removed from a direct sales role.

After all, in any firm employing more than just a few sales staff, someone must serve as a sales manager. In smaller companies, this may involve a single position. In larger firms, any number of people may serve as sales managers or hold related administrative or executive positions.

Sales managers' duties vary, but in addition to those mentioned above, they also may include assigning territories, establishing or coordinating training programs, and maintaining contacts with dealers and distributors. They hire and supervise sales staff and, in some cases, provide management oversight for other sales mangers as well as support staff. Other duties include supporting sales staff though professional development activities and advising them on effective performance, analyzing sales-related data, compiling reports, determining inventory needs, and overseeing efforts to keep customers satisfied.

Those who move into sales management positions may look toward the possibility of a bright future. In general, a promotion from a sales job to one with management responsibilities is an indication that higher level managers believe an employee has already been doing a good job and also holds the potential for performing well in a management role. Then if this newly assigned manager lives up to expectations, continued job advancement is a distinct possibility. This may consist of promotion to higher-level sales management positions or it might include movement into other management roles outside of the sales area. In such instances, successful sales managers use their experience as a bridge to other, nonsales roles. They take on other positions in marketing, financial management, or general management. It is not uncommon to find men or women who started out as salespersons and eventually worked their way up to positions as company vice presidents or presidents.

Others use their skills and experience as background for teaching, consulting, starting their own businesses, or other paths to career success.

CHAPTER 3

COMPUTER, ELECTRONIC, AND ELECTRICAL EQUIPMENT SALES

Like it or not, we live in a world dominated by the use of electrical equipment and electronic devices. From the moment your clock radio rouses you from bed to that last dose of late-night television, electrical and electronic products play a major role in your life. Computers, televisions, lighting systems, automobile components, CD players, cash registers, and countless other devices and systems are commonplace examples of the importance played by such items in daily life. At home, at work or school, and everywhere else, electrical and electronic products are in high demand.

Certainly, this area represents big business—very big business, in fact. According to the U.S. Department of Commerce, American manufacturers produce more than $180 billion worth of electronic equipment annually. That is more than the gross national product of most nations! Add to this the products manufactured in other nations but sold by American representatives, not to mention the huge volume of sales of related products and services, and scope of this business area is truly daunting.

In any field this large, plenty of career opportunities await those with the right combination of skills, knowledge, and motivation. This is certainly true in the area of sales. The marketing of electrical and electronic products and the demand for computer equipment, communication devices, and countless other products provides fertile ground for qualified technical sales professionals.

In addition to items such as computers, television sets, and audio equipment, the electronics industry produces a wide variety of goods for business, military, or consumer use. This includes not only complete electronic devices but also components incorporated within other products ranging from appliances to airplanes.

Computer-related products include semiconductors as well as items such as printers, scanners, disk drives and other storage devices, input devices, and other peripherals and supplies. Other electronic products include calculating and accounting machines, cell phones and other communications equipment, and military equipment including radar and missile guidance systems.

Companies specializing in these and other products come in all varieties. Some are large, multinational corporations offering an array of products and employing tens of thousands of people. Others are midsized companies providing a less diverse product mix. Some are relatively small firms specializing in just a few products.

INDUSTRY TRENDS

A major focus of this industry is innovation. Although all industries face change, the electronics industry changes at a particularly rapid pace. This makes it a highly competitive one, as manufacturers are constantly coming up with new and improved products. As a result, sales personnel face special challenges. Not only must they keep up with new technical advances developed by their own employers, but the competitive nature of the field also requires that they be knowledgeable about the developments of competitors and about new trends in the field.

The industry also tends to have a positive image and a work environment many find appealing. Although sales personnel in any industry generally enjoy a different working environment than production workers, they are also a part of the overall environment. In the computer and electronics arena, this includes clean laboratory and production facilities as well as the progressive image engendered by the "high tech" label.

According to the U.S. Department of Labor, the electronic equipment manufacturing industry employed about 1.6 million people in 1998. About 13 percent of these workers held administrative, clerical, or sales jobs.

About thirteen thousand companies specialize in manufacturing of electronic products. The largest single component consisted of companies offering electronic components and accessories (43 percent), followed by those providing computer and office equipment (24 percent), communication equipment (18 percent), search and navigation equipment (10 percent), and household audio and video equipment (5 percent).

TYPES OF SALES OPPORTUNITIES

Sales-related job opportunities vary widely in the computer, electronics, and electrical industries. They range from introductory jobs requiring minimal training or experience to high-level executive positions, and include a variety of specialized roles.

Entry-Level Positions

Many entry-level jobs in this area focus on retail sales, customer service, or other functions that are important but do not necessarily require advanced skill levels. They can be great starting points for young workers or those wishing to break into the field.

Here is a position description for an entry-level position with a major manufacturer of computer peripherals:

Position: Customer Service Representative

Job expectations: responding to customer inquiries in a call center environment, performing data entry, providing detailed product information, solving problems and maintaining customer satisfaction, effectively navigating multiple information databases, routing inquiries to proper departments or individuals as appropriate

Requirements: associate degree and/or related job experience

Other jobs appropriate for beginners include a retail sales clerk, working in a store specializing in consumer electronics products; a sales associate, functioning as a trainee for a manufacturer of industrial electrical equipment; or a telephone sales representative, working for a firm providing home-based electronic security devices.

Mid-Level Positions

In a mid-level sales position, job knowledge is often more important than a specified number of years of experience, especially where highly technical products are being offered. For example, consider a sales professional specializing in software designed to help companies save disk space on servers used for networked computers.

To be successful in such a position, an individual would need to be well versed in the features of storage-related products, techniques for evaluating the storage management needs of customers, and advantages provided by the software being marketed. This would require a basic understanding of server environments and available software tools, which is normally obtained through previous experience as a network administrator, sales engineer, or support engineer. In many cases, the actual amount of time spent in such roles would be less important than the basic competencies involved. This would include an ability to "speak the lingo" expected of those with knowledge in such areas.

Here is a description for a mid-level sales position specializing in software used by nonprofit organizations to track charitable contributions:

Title: Regional Sales Specialist

Requirements: at least two years of sales experience; bachelor's degree required with a major in business, accounting, or information systems preferred

Position overview: responsible for coordinating sales of donor relations and accounting software packages to colleges, universities, hospitals, social service agencies, and other nonprofit organizations

Territory: southwestern United States sales area

Traits desired: team player, ability to meet preestablished sales goals and revenue targets, skill in helping clients make sound decisions for obtaining and implementing software solutions, willingness to travel as necessary within assigned territory, ability to maintain home-based office, excellent communication skills, proven organizational abilities

Other mid-level sales positions generally require a significant level of previous sales experience, typically in a directly related area. A bachelor's degree is also a common requirement. Such jobs represent a step up from entry-level jobs, and as such can provide solid career potential. In turn, they also can provide ambitious sales professionals with a route for continued career advancement.

Senior-Level Positions

Of course, senior-level jobs normally require substantial previous experience. For example, a major software provider recently advertised for a vice president of sales. This position was responsible for developing and managing a successful sales team, as well as designing overall sales strategies. The successful applicant was expected to have at least ten years of sales experience with corporate customers, including substantial experience in sales management. Those with previous experience in a combination of enterprise software sales, sales to service, start-up experience, and at least five years in sales management were preferred.

Senior-level positions provide the ultimate in job potential. In areas such as computer systems, software, or other "high tech" sales, senior personnel may enjoy excellent salaries, enviable benefits, and all the "perks" that may come with executive positions. Naturally, competition for such jobs can be intense, and performance expectations are high. But for those who are successful at this level, the rewards can be impressive.

PROFILE: A COMPUTER SALES PROFESSIONAL

Matt is a sales associate for a company specializing in electronic projection devices used to make presentations in classrooms, business meetings, and other environments. He enjoys working in a field where products are changing rapidly, and there is a sense of excitement about being on the "cutting edge" of technology. At the same time, he appreciates the fact that the products he works with can be used and understood by virtually anyone.

Matt majored in marketing in college, and he developed good communication skills through classes in business writing, public speaking, and other subjects. He also worked part-time in an office products store, honing customer relations skills in the process.

After graduating he took a telemarketing position for a credit card company, but he did not enjoy the work. Then when an opportunity developed with his current employer, he interviewed, was offered the job, and began working as a trainee. Soon he was in the field operating as a full-fledged sales professional.

In this job, Matt is responsible for direct sales of company products. This involves calling on prospective customers, putting on product demonstrations, and providing technical details and other product information for customers or prospective customers. In reviewing sales options with customers, he also is responsible for quoting appropriate prices and executing the necessary paperwork or electronic documents for each sale made.

One reality of the job that at first seemed imposing, if not downright threatening, was that Matt was expected to meet a monthly sales quota. His employer made it clear from the start that this was expected as a condition for continued employment. But once on the job, Matt quickly learned that the quota was a reasonable one. Today he is earning a solid income and planning to continue in the field. He finds the combination of working with people and handling useful technical products to be a source of continuing job enrichment.

FUTURE PROSPECTS

Ask anybody anywhere about job prospects related to computers or electronics, and you're almost certain to get a positive answer. Even those who are not especially well informed about the world of high technology are generally aware that this is a "hot" area.

Certainly there is much more to it than this simple assessment, but there is no doubt that a future in the area of computers, electronics, or electrical products holds great promise for many workers. This includes a significant need for those who are both qualified and motivated to function as sales professionals.

CHAPTER 4

PHARMACEUTICAL AND CHEMICAL SALES

For most people, the word "technical" evokes images of equipment such as computers or other advanced electronic devices. But many other products fall under the umbrella of advanced technology, including prescription drugs, industrial chemicals, and other products based on the work of engineers, scientists, and other highly trained specialists.

Typically, the beginning for such products is a laboratory or other research setting, where researchers develop new or improved materials that might prove of benefit to business customers or consumers. When a new product is perfected and then a commercial need for it established, the process moves from one of product development to marketing. Then sales personnel begin to play their role. Using their knowledge of available products and their skills in the sales process, they form the bridge between manufacturers, wholesalers or retailers, and buyers.

Accomplished sales professionals play a key role in the pharmaceutical and chemical industries. They help customers make informed decisions while representing the needs of their employers to make a profit.

PHARMACEUTICAL SALES

The drug manufacturing industry plays a truly important role in modern society. Its products improve the lives of millions of people, in many cases literally making the difference between life and death, and in others allowing people to overcome illnesses or injuries that would otherwise greatly diminish their quality of life.

Name a disease or infirmity, and there are numerous drugs to help cure or control it. From cardiovascular disease to asthma, from pneumonia to diabetes, from sore throats to sunburn—no matter what the health challenge, sophisticated drugs are available to diminish the negative effects involved.

According to the U.S. Department of Labor, the drug industry includes about 1,700 manufacturers and related employers. They employ about 300,000 workers, some 40 percent of whom work for large companies employing at least 1,000 people. Their products include both pharmaceutical preparations and finished drugs as well as serums and vaccines, bulk chemicals, and diagnostic products.

Sales positions play an important part in this industry. About 6,000 people are employed in marketing and sales. Many fill roles as pharmaceutical sales representatives. They maintain communications between their companies and existing and potential clients. It is their duty to represent their company's products to customers such as physicians, pharmacists, dentists, and health care administrators.

In most cases, employers in this area require that sales representatives hold bachelor's degrees. Those with backgrounds in chemistry, biology, or other scientific disciplines tend to have the strongest chance for employment, although this is not always an absolute requirement. Most companies also offer comprehensive training programs for sales personnel to acquaint them fully with the products being sold.

From a career stance, a strong point with the pharmaceutical industry is that it seems to have a very bright future. Government projections place it among the fastest growing manufacturing industries for the next decade, and demand for its products will almost certainly continue to grow as the population grows and as people enjoy longer life spans. New developments in medical research and the growing importance of biotechnological research also hold promise for the future of this industry.

A variety of companies manufacture or sell pharmaceutical products. Some of the companies in this area include:

Abbott Laboratories
American Home Products
Amgen
Bayer Corporation
Bristol-Myers Squibb
Elan Pharmaceuticals
Johnson & Johnson
Knoll Pharmaceutical Company
Lilly
Merck
Novartis
Ortho-McNeil
Pfizer
3M Pharmaceuticals

Types of Pharmaceutical Sales Positions

Virtually every major manufacturer in this industry employs large numbers of sales personnel. For example, a recent examination of the website of Merck, a major pharmaceutical manufacturer, revealed that more than thirty positions were open in the area of sales and marketing. They included positions such as Clinical Account Executive, Product Manager, Arthritis and Anti-Inflammatory Specialty Representative, Neuroscience Specialty Representative, and Professional Representative. Others included Hospital Sales Representative, Product

Manager, Business Manager for Sales, Installation Account Coordinator, and Director of Product Management.

Some of these positions were headquartered in Franklin Lakes, New Jersey. Others were for locations such as Kansas City, Missouri; Phoenix, Arizona; Des Moines, Iowa; and Madison, Wisconsin.

A similar examination of job openings with corporate giant Pfizer showed scores of job openings in sales and related areas. Position titles for job vacancies included Healthcare Representative, Healthcare Representative I, Key Account Manager, Account Manager, Regional Account Manager, Territory Manager, Associate Director of Sales and Marketing Operations, Forecast Analyst, Field Force Effectiveness Director, Sales Planning Manager, Category Tactical Planner, Partnership Manager-Field Sales, Global Customer Analyst, and Associate Manager of Sales Analysis.

Locations for these jobs included San Francisco; Towson, Maryland; Philadelphia; La Jolla, California; Hackensack and Plainfield, New Jersey; Spokane, Washington; Lynchburg, Virginia; Anchorage, Alaska; and Grand Rapids, Michigan; among others.

Here is a typical job description for a pharmaceutical sales position:

Job title: Sales Representative

Location: Richmond, Virginia and Virginia–North Carolina area

Duties: developing and managing business relationships with targeted therapeutic specialists and customers focusing on the promotion of specified products

Required skills: two years related experience demonstrating sales skills, technical knowledge of the therapeutic area, communication skills, leadership ability, account management experience, project management experience, self-motivation and initiative, ability to work independently

Education: bachelor's degree required with major preferred in natural sciences, business, or a health-related field

Other pharmaceutical sales positions tend to have similar responsibilities, although, of course, details vary according to the level of job involved, the products being offered, and other fundamental considerations.

Typical responsibilities include the following:

- conducting market analyses
- identifying growth areas
- tracking market trends
- developing business plans
- defining and/or covering assigned sales territories
- maintaining appropriate equipment and supplies
- storing, transporting, and disseminating product samples
- maintaining detailed records
- coordinating sales efforts with fellow sales personnel
- contacting and maintaining relationships with customers
- attending sales meetings
- participating in training or professional development activities
- negotiating sales contracts
- performing customer relations and follow-up tasks

CHEMICAL SALES

Another major area in which sales personnel deal with technical products is the chemical industry. Sales professionals in this area sell products manufactured by chemical companies, raw materials necessary for various manufacturing processes, plastics, agricultural chemicals, laboratory and production supplies, and other products.

Most sales professionals in this field represent chemical manufacturers, distributors, or other employers. They typically do not sell directly to consumers, but instead operate on a business-to-business relationship.

Types of Chemical Sales Positions

As in other highly technical areas, the chemical industry requires specialized knowledge of those who work in the field. In many cases, sales personnel have a background in chemistry or chemical engineering. Those who have a more general business background also may find a place in chemical sales, but they may need to acquire specialized vocabulary and develop an understanding of complex products or processes.

In any case, most jobs share certain basic responsibilities. For example, a major chemical company lists the following roles and responsibilities for account managers:

- serve as solutions consultants for customers
- provide an interface with people in customer organizations
- foster long-term supplier partnerships
- implement growth strategies with client companies
- carry out development strategies for new account possibilities

Here is a position description for an external sales position with a large chemical company:

Position: Technical Sales Specialist

Location: Chicago and four Midwestern states

Job responsibilities: making sales calls to customers and potential customers, providing sales forecasts, developing new accounts, maintaining accounts with existing customers, establishing and maintaining positive relationships with customers, completing weekly and monthly reports, performing other related duties

Qualifications: bachelor's degree in chemistry or engineering; one to four years of related job experience preferred

The following job description covers the basic responsibilities for a position with an East Coast manufacturer of chemical production equipment:

Position: Account Representative

Duties: identify and qualify prospective clients, prepare and deliver presentations, conduct equipment demonstrations, prepare price quotations, negotiate sales terms, coordinate delivery and installation of equipment, arrange for customer training in using equipment, provide follow-up and maintain client relationships, compile sales data and complete sales reports, provide related duties

Qualifications: bachelor's degree required; degree in chemistry or engineering preferred; at least one year of sales experience required; technical sales experience preferred

Related Roles

Other positions in chemical sales range from those of sales engineers to sales managers, as well as those with other defined sales functions. Too, some positions specialize in equipment rather than drugs or chemical products. For example, a job might focus on selling the sophisticated balances employed in weighing chemicals used in laboratory analysis. Another might sell chromatography or other laboratory or analytical equipment or instruments.

PROFILE: A CHEMICAL SALES PROFESSIONAL

For Tim, a career in chemistry was a lifelong goal, and at age twenty-eight he had been employed as a practicing chemist for more than four years. But in spending time with his best friend, a successful executive in the financial products industry, Tim began to see some of the advantages of a sales career. He envied the fact that his friend spent much of his time in different environments, calling on clients and traveling to different cities. His own job, on the other hand, required him to put in long hours, day after day, in the same laboratory setting. Tim also found himself yearning for more contact with other people. A naturally gregarious person, he enjoyed meeting new people, something his current position seldom involved.

Aware of these feelings, Tim's friend suggested that he make a career change. Why not enroll in some business classes and take a shot at selling financial services? Tim thought about it, but he wasn't sure if that would be a good move. In addition, he hated the thought of entirely abandoning the field in which he had worked so hard and had gained a wealth of specialized knowledge.

Then it occurred to him: Why not check out the possibility of working in the chemical industry in a sales capacity? He talked with a couple of sales professionals, did some background research on major chemical manufacturers, and decided that might be a reasonable move. So Tim updated his resume and began applying for sales positions in the industry.

He was disappointed at first when employers expressed little interest, and he feared that his lack of sales experience might prevent him from making any progress in this direction. But then he got an interview, did well in the interviewing process, and landed a sales position. The job offer was contingent upon completion of a company-sponsored training program, but Tim gladly accepted. He pored over manuals, watched videotapes, and participated in training sessions. Then he began his job as an entry-level salesperson.

Today, Tim is a highly successful sales professional. He received two promotions in his first three years on the job and then took a position with another company where his track record has continued to be a sterling one.

Tim says that his path is certainly not right for everyone, but it has worked out well for him. He travels frequently, but the amount of travel is not so extensive that it has become burdensome. At the same time, he finds the sales process stimulating and has become knowledgeable in areas of the industry about which he knew little before going into sales. He also has started working on a master's in business administration (M.B.A.) degree, going to school during the evenings and taking a number of courses through distance learning so that his sales and travel responsibilities do not keep him from meeting educational requirements. He plans to continue in sales, although he also is thinking about the possibility of moving into executive management. When asked if he is glad he made the switch into sales, Tim's answer is a definite "yes."

FUTURE PROSPECTS

With changing economic conditions, career prospects in any one industry vary from year to year. During economic downturns, for example, many chemical companies may reduce their workforce, and then expand when business conditions improve. But in the foreseeable future, significant demand will continue for sales personnel in both the chemical and pharmaceutical industries. Particularly with the latter, the combination of population growth, longer life spans, and increased demand for medicines—along with the continued development of new drugs and applications—will lead to growing needs for qualified sales professionals.

CHAPTER 5

BIOLOGICAL AND BIOTECHNOLOGY SALES

In recent years, amazing advances have taken place in the biological sciences. Developments in everything from growing bigger tomatoes to prolonging human life have come at a rapid pace, not to mention the potential offered by breakthroughs in understanding the basic genetics behind life itself.

At one time, it could be expected that most such advances would be restricted to the laboratories of a small cadre of scientists, with only occasional breakthroughs reaching the general public. But more recently, advancing knowledge has resulted in many practical applications. As a result, commercial potential in the biological sciences is enormous, with a need for qualified sales personnel constituting an important part of the picture.

BIOTECHNOLOGY SALES

An area of growing potential for a variety of careers, including those in sales, is biotechnology. This is an area of science dealing with molecular and cellular biology; plant, animal, and human genetics; and how the human immune system fights disease. A major focus is on practical applications rather than simply on theoretical research.

According to the Biotechnology Industries Association (BIO), more than two hundred million people worldwide have already been helped by the more than eighty biotechnology drug products and vaccines approved by the U.S. Food and Drug Administration. In addition, hundreds of other biotechnology drug products and vaccines are currently in development. Such products address a variety of illnesses and needs including heart disease, cancer, Alzheimer's disease, and multiple sclerosis, among others.

Biotechnology products include home pregnancy tests and other diagnostic products, improved foods, biopesticides and other agricultural products, environmental products, and products used in industrial areas ranging from chemicals to metal and mineral production.

According to BIO, more than 1,200 biotechnology companies now operate in the United States, employing more than 150,000 people. In 1998, sales in the biotechnology industry exceeded $13 billion.

With the growing importance of biotechnology, opportunities in related areas, including sales, are promising. Responsibilities are not unlike those for sales positions described in previous chapters, but with a focus on the biological sciences.

Here is a position description for a sales position with a major biotechnology firm:

Position: Biotech Sales Specialist

Duties: demonstrating and selling designated biotechnology products; maintaining positive relationships with existing and potential customers; answering customer inquiries and resolving problems; preparing call reports, sales forecasts, and other reports; achieving and maintaining technical proficiency and knowledge for all products represented; developing and keeping track of sales leads

Special considerations: frequent travel required, including substantial overnight travel

Qualifications: bachelor's degree or higher in biochemistry, biology, or other natural science; at least two years of previous sales experience—biotechnology or related area preferred

Here is another description for a sales job specializing in biotechnology products:

Title: Sales Executive

Location: Atlanta, Georgia, and southern United States

Duties: identifying, qualifying, and closing new customers and product-related sales opportunities

Specific tasks: implementing tactical marketing campaigns to increase sales of genetically modified agricultural products, developing and implementing regional business area plans, providing advice and assistance to technical staff regarding marketing potential for new products, developing and implementing appropriate marketing tactics to maintain existing customer relationships

Required qualifications: bachelor's degree in biology or related field, along with at least two years successful sales experience

Preferred skills: excellent communication skills and good organizational competencies; must be willing to travel throughout designated territory

Other Sales Positions

Other sales positions related to the life sciences have a similar focus. As with other industries, they include entry-level, mid-level, and upper-level jobs and cover areas ranging from inside sales to sales management. Products sometimes overlap with those sold in the pharmaceutical or chemical industries, and they also may include other areas such as specimens for laboratory research, supplies for medical testing, agricultural products, and environmental products and services.

Some sales personnel in this general area may specialize in selling equipment for biological or medical applications. This may consist of equipment in any number of specialty areas such as orthopedics, neurosurgery, cardiovascular surgery, or ophthalmic surgery.

PROFILE: A BIOTECHNOLOGY SALES PROFESSIONAL

Like many students, Annette started out with one set of career goals and then switched to another. When she was in high school, Annette found she had a flair for science and did well in courses such as biology and chemistry. At the same time, she had a love of dogs, cats, and other animals. Considering these factors, she decided that a career as a veterinarian might be a good path to take. So Annette enrolled in college and declared a major in biology. Her plan was to do as well as possible in her undergraduate studies and then apply for admission to veterinary school.

As she learned more about the veterinary field, however, Annette began to question whether it was the right choice for her. When she took a summer job in a veterinary hospital, her doubts were confirmed. She enjoyed interacting with the people who brought in their pets, but found she really did not like most of the tasks involved in working directly with animals.

At that point, Annette began the process of switching career goals. She decided to complete a degree in biology and then seek a job, but she wasn't sure just what type of position to pursue. Then during her senior year, she began attending job fairs and researching prospective jobs for biology graduates.

When a company specializing in biological products granted her an interview, she was not interested at first because it mentioned sales, and she had never considered that option. But then as things progressed, she thought the job sounded potentially interesting. Company personnel explained that she would be trained in sales at the onset and that she would be dealing with concepts she had mastered as a biology major.

So she decided to give it a try. And somewhat to her surprise, she found the job both challenging and enjoyable. Within a year, Annette was operating with confidence and a high degree of capability, selling biopesticides and related products. She has taken additional classes in sales strategies and techniques and has received excellent performance evaluations. Today, she is enjoying a career as a successful technical sales professional.

FUTURE PROSPECTS

It has been said that while the late twentieth century might be designated the age of the computer, the twenty-first will be the age of biology. Every day, it seems, we hear of some new discovery in genetics, bioengineering, or some other area related to the life sciences. At the same time, new companies are being formed to deal with commercial applications of biological research and development, and existing firms are continuing with similar efforts.

While this may be great news for those interested in scientific careers, the same can be said for important support areas such as sales. The marketing and sales of biological products will provide solid careers for many workers in the years ahead.

CHAPTER 6

OTHER TECHNICAL SALES

The previous chapters have covered some of the major areas in which technical sales professionals work. But they are not the only relevant job areas. Other industries and organizations meeting a variety of needs also provide employment possibilities for those specializing in technical sales.

Most professionals in these areas focus on one of the following functions: sales, sales management, marketing, or marketing management. Others work in related areas ranging from accounting to general management. Major industries in which they work include aerospace manufacturing, motor vehicle and equipment manufacturing, telecommunications, and other areas.

AEROSPACE MANUFACTURING

The aerospace manufacturing industry is an area in which the skills of technical sales professionals definitely come into play. This industry includes companies that produce airplanes and other types of aircraft, engines and other components, guided missiles, space vehicles, and related products. Also included are companies specializing in research, development, repair or modification of aircraft, space vehicles, and the systems and components related to their operation.

The largest segment of the aerospace industry is made up of companies that produce aircraft or major components such as engines or navigation systems. Often these products are further divided into two major segments: civil aircraft or military aircraft.

The majority of companies in the civil aircraft area produce transport aircraft for civilian use. Their products include everything from small, turboprop airplanes to huge jets used by air cargo firms or commercial airlines. Some companies specialize in smaller airplanes for general aviation use such as small planes flown by private individuals or corporate jets employed by companies for business transportation. Another segment consists of civil helicopters for use by private companies, police departments, emergency medical services, and others.

A significant area in this industry is the construction of military aircraft for use by the U.S. military or for the military services of other nations who purchase such products. These products range from fighter planes, bombers, and others designed for air defense or offensive warfare, to large planes used for transporting equipment or troops.

Another segment of this industry produces guided missiles, space vehicles, propulsion units, and related products. This includes both equipment used for military applications and products utilized in civilian space exploration efforts. The latter consists primarily of needs of the National Aeronautic and Space Administration, but also includes some privately funded programs. Increasingly, such products are being used not just for exploring space but for practical applications such as communications satellites.

According to the U.S. Department of Labor, the aerospace industry includes about eighteen hundred companies employing more than six hundred thousand people. By far the great majority (about 95 percent) focus on the aircraft and parts sector, with the remainder producing guided missiles, space vehicles, and related products. Most employers are large companies, with a majority employing more than one thousand workers.

The largest single customer in this industry is the federal government. Other customers include airlines, cargo transportation companies, foreign governments, and large corporations.

Much of the purchasing in this industry is done through competitive bidding. This shapes much of the work of sales personnel, but their role is still an important one. Sales and marketing professionals help companies identify markets and make a case for the purchase of their products.

MOTOR VEHICLE AND EQUIPMENT MANUFACTURING

Technical sales professionals fulfill a variety of roles in the motor vehicle and equipment manufacturing industry. Motor vehicles are very complex, with sophisticated systems, subsystems, and components making up any single car, truck, or other vehicle. The buying and selling of these various products creates fertile opportunities for sales professionals with the necessary level of technical understanding.

After all, this industry is one of the largest in the world. In the United States alone, more than 180 million cars and trucks are now in operation. In Canada, the automotive industry is a major employer. In other nations around the globe, the number of motor vehicles continues to grow.

Those who sell cars are part of the sales world, but one might not consider them technical sales professionals when compared with those dealing with other advanced technologies. But the finished cars and trucks sold to consumers are only a part of this industry. According to the Department of Labor, more than fifty-three hundred firms manufacture motor vehicles or related equipment, including companies specializing in small parts or other components. In addition, thousands of stores specialize in selling auto parts to consumers or businesses. With both manufacturers and retail stores, the need exists for trained sales staff to market products such as axles, brakes, engines, radiators, steering mechanisms, transmissions, lighting systems, and other items.

Well over one million people are employed in motor vehicle and equipment manufacturing in the United States and Canada. Although the majority of jobs consist of production-related positions, personnel in sales and marketing also play important roles. Add to that the thousands of sales personnel who work in auto parts stores or related businesses, including not just part-time or temporary staff but retail managers who pursue a full-time career track in this area.

In addition to positions involving direct sales, related jobs include those of purchasing agents and managers. Those positions are responsible for buying raw materials, machinery, tools, and other equipment needed to produce the motor vehicles and parts, or for buying previously assembled vehicle components.

PRINTING AND PUBLISHING

The printing and publishing industry reaches everyone's lives. From books, newspapers, and magazines to the labels on food containers or merchandise packaging, printed material is everywhere. Because the printing of such material can involve sophisticated printing equipment and services, some sales personnel in this industry also can be considered technical sales professionals.

The printing and publishing industry includes a number of segments such as commercial printing establishments, newspapers, and greeting card companies. Many companies consist of small printing shops, but some larger firms also exist. Sales opportunities in the industry include both the sale of printing services and those who market printing equipment and related products.

The U.S. Department of Labor reports that more than 1.5 million people are employed in the printing and publishing industry. In addition to commercial printing, they work in areas such as book printing, production of business forms, plate making services, and magazine publishing.

About 10 percent of workers hold positions in marketing or sales. Additional employees serve as sales or marketing managers.

In recent years, the printing industry has become increasingly "high tech" in nature, with growing use of computers and other advanced technologies. In addition, more and more segments of the publishing industry now produce products electronically. This advancing level of technological sophistication in the industry has required sales personnel to acquire and use many of the skills typical of sales personnel in other highly technical areas.

TELECOMMUNICATIONS

Significant advances in the telecommunications industry have changed it drastically in recent years. Where once it focused on traditional voice telephone communication, the industry now has expanded into data, graphics, and video communications. This includes the burgeoning use of mobile, hand-held devices including cell phones, personal digital assistants, and other devices used in wireless communications. Both technological advancements and changes in government regulation have fostered new growth and competition in this industry.

The highly technical nature of telephone networks, new devices for wireless communication, and expanding wireless services, such as paging, satellite telephone services, and mobile access to the World Wide Web, have all brought opportunities for technically oriented salespersons. Although many sales positions in this industry deal with nontechnical areas (such as selling long-distance telephone plans to consumers), others cover products ranging from advanced equipment to consulting services for designing a company's communications infrastructure. The process of informing potential customers about such products and handling sales transactions requires the work of appropriately prepared technical sales professionals.

In addition, the industry includes such segments as E-mail, facsimile, and other message communications services as well as the operation of radar stations and short-range radio networks.

On an overall basis, the telecommunications industry employs slightly more than one million people, according to government employment studies, with the largest single employment area being telephone communications. About 109,000 people work in marketing and sales.

Many sales personnel focus on selling telecommunications services including long distance telephone service, personal answering services, voice mail, and electronic mail. The level of technical expertise varies, with those serving businesses rather than consumers often involved in more complex sales transactions.

BIOMETRICS

A rapidly emerging area is that of biometrics. According to the International Biometric Industry Association, biometrics represents an emerging area in which biological information can be used, through the use of specially designed devices, as a means of safeguarding personal information, preventing identity theft, and supporting security.

Through the use of advanced hardware and software, biometric devices create electronic templates that are stored and then compared to live images when the need occurs to verify a person's identity. This approach is becoming an increasingly common alternative to traditional methods of confirming identity such as showing a driver's license, birth certificate, or other form of identification. It can be used to help protect against credit card theft and unauthorized use, network hacking, and other illegal activities.

As this technology becomes more prevalent, opportunities for sales personnel are likely to increase. As in other areas of advanced technology, appropriately prepared sales staff will be needed to explain product advantages and help customers in selecting biometric devices or related services.

RELATED JOBS

Some jobs not directly involved in sales have responsibilities that are somewhat similar. Such positions represent alternative possibilities for experienced sales professionals who decide to explore other career paths, as well as students or newcomers who prefer them to actual sales career tracks.

For example, operating at the other end of the sales process from salespersons are purchasing managers, buyers, and purchasing agents. Workers in these roles purchase merchandise for their employers. In the process, they attempt to obtain the lowest prices possible while ensuring that products are of sufficient quality to meet their needs. Their work may include selecting suppliers of the goods or services, negotiating prices, and processing contracts.

Persons who hold these roles may be called by any of a number of titles. Frequently used position titles include "purchasing director," "purchasing manager," "purchasing agent," "buyer," "industrial buyer," and "contract specialist." In some organizations, the term "purchasing manager" refers to a higher-level position than does "buyer" or "purchasing agent." When this difference is recognized, the latter tends to refer to those performing more routine tasks, while the former is reserved for those who handle more complex duties, in some cases including supervising purchasing agents within the same organization.

Advertising, marketing, and public relations managers also work in areas related to sales. These areas may provide employment potential for sales personnel interested in material recording, scheduling, dispatching, and distributing occupations.

SELF-EMPLOYMENT

Another possibility for successful sales professionals is self-employment. Brokers who have developed connections through previous employment, for instance, might start their own wholesale brokerage businesses. Using relationships and contact information obtained through previous experience and taking advantage of appropriate software, on-line communications, and other high technologies, they might build successful businesses. Similarly, those with other types of sales experiences may develop their own sales, marketing, consulting, or service firms.

CHAPTER 7

EDUCATIONAL PREPARATION

In the competitive world of the twenty-first century workplace, the importance of education cannot be overstated. Whether this means educational credentials earned in advance of employment or training completed on the job, education is a key ingredient in career success for sales professionals.

Just what type of educational preparation is needed for a career in technical sales? Actually, requirements vary widely. Some jobs require little or no training beyond high school; others may require a college degree. In some cases, degree requirements are specific to areas such as engineering; in others, a degree in business, marketing, or a less specific area (such as liberal arts) is acceptable.

Often, new employees undergo training offered by the employer or provided by trade associations, professional training firms, or other parties. Typical topics include effective selling techniques, management strategies, and use of electronic information systems.

BASIC EDUCATIONAL REQUIREMENTS

An attractive feature of sales-related occupations is that no single, specific set of educational qualifications exists. In technical areas, the most common expectation is a bachelor's degree in a business field or in a technical field related to the products or services being offered.

For some other positions an associate (two-year) degree, or a combination of education and experience, may be expected.

In many cases, a high school diploma is sufficient for an entry-level position, especially in retail sales. Typically, a new hire with minimal educational credentials will complete company-sponsored training at the onset of employment. With many employers, those with additional education also may be expected to participate in similar training.

Typical college majors of those who become employed in technical sales include the following. However, it should be noted that with the breadth of possibilities in what might be considered technical sales careers today, these represent just a sample of some of the majors that would help prepare students for employment in sales-related occupations.

business administration
marketing
management
advertising
public relations
economics
computer science
engineering
chemistry
biology

BEGINNING THE EDUCATIONAL PROCESS

Few high school students choose a future career in sales while still in high school. Typically, such a decision is made after high school graduation, either during the job search process or while in college.

For those who plan to attend college, the usual steps in achieving this goal include selecting a college or university, obtaining financial aid or other necessary resources, enrolling in college, selecting an appropriate major or course of study, and enhancing the college experience through internships, part-time or summer employment, or other experiences.

Selecting a College or University

The first step in obtaining a college degree is selecting the right school for you. In making such a choice, the U.S. Department of Education suggests considering the following factors: available courses and types of programs, admissions requirements, academic quality, price, services, and activities.

For any college in which you're interested, check out these and other details as covered in its catalog or other publications. Much information is also available via the Internet, not only through any college's official website but also through descriptions provided by other sources. Also consider such factors as evidence that the college is fully accredited, the school's job placement rates, and the availability of scholarships or other financial aid.

Before committing to any college, be sure to visit the campus at least once and obtain a firsthand look at classroom facilities, the library, and other features. In the process, keep in mind that while selecting a college is important, it is not necessarily a permanent decision. If you change your mind later, you can always transfer to another institution. So don't let the selection process cause undue stress.

Funding College Costs

Along with the process of selecting a college, be sure to explore all available options for paying educational expenses. Attending college is an expensive proposition, involving the payment of tuition, room and board or commuting expenses, book costs, and a variety of other fees. Total costs may range from $1,000 to $3,000 yearly at a community college to more than $30,000 yearly at many private four-year colleges. Considering the scope of such costs, some form of financial assistance will be of interest to most students.

A wide range of financial aid possibilities exists for students who need support to attend college. This includes scholarships, grants, loans, and other types of aid offered by the federal government, state governments, private organizations, and colleges and universities themselves. Federal government aid, which constitutes the single largest source of student assistance, includes the following:

Grants: These include both Pell grants and FSEOG (Federal Supplemental Educational Opportunity Grants). Grants are outright awards that, unlike loans, need not be repaid. Pell grants may be awarded to undergraduate students who have not earned bachelors' or professional degrees. They are based on financial need, with the neediest students obtaining the largest awards. FSEOG are grants for undergraduates with exceptional financial need and may be awarded to students who have also received Pell grants.

Work-study: The federal work-study program provides part-time jobs for undergraduate and graduate students who demonstrate financial need. The program provides a source of financial assistance along with the opportunity to gain work experience while still in school.

Loans: Government loans include Federal Perkins loans, Stafford loans, and PLUS loans. Undergraduate or graduate students with exceptional financial need may receive Perkins loans. Although the funds must be repaid, thanks to government backing, the interest rate is lower than most other types of loans.

Stafford loans are offered directly to students through the William D. Ford Direct Loan Program and are available to those who may not qualify for other types of aid as well as to needier students. Their advantages include an interest rate that is lower than most commercial loans and a long repayment period.

PLUS loans, which are available to parents, also are available along with several other programs.

To see if you qualify for federal student aid, you must first complete a detailed application. You may submit the Free Application for Federal Student Aid (FAFSA) electronically from your home computer or from a computer at a central location. You also can submit a paper application in English or Spanish.

More information is available from:

Federal Student Aid Information Center
P.O. Box 84
Washington, DC 20044
1-800/4-FED-AID (1-800/433-3243)

For on-line information, check out the U.S. Department of Education home page at www.fafsa.ed.gov.

Along with government aid, be sure to pursue other sources of aid. Scholarships offered by colleges, privately funded scholarships, and state-sponsored student aid programs are all worth checking out.

For more details about sources of student aid, consult sources such as the U.S. Department of Education home page, other websites about financial aid and scholarships, college financial aid offices, high school guidance counselors, and financial aid directories available in libraries and bookstores.

Using the College Experience to Prepare for Employment

Once you enroll in college, the courses you select, along with other positive experiences, will be important in building credentials needed for career success. For students anticipating a sales career, key steps will include choosing a major in an appropriate academic area, developing strong oral communication skills, and building experience through extracurricular activities, summer employment, or other activities. Also important is building a track record of academic success and personal development that will look attractive to potential employers.

COLLEGE AND UNIVERSITY SALES PROGRAMS

If you decide to take the route of majoring in business or a related area, or even more specifically in sales or marketing, you may choose from a variety of programs. Not all postsecondary schools offer such programs, but many do.

Following is an overview of representative sales-related programs offered at four-year colleges and universities.

Kennesaw State University

A good example of a broad-based academic approach in this area is the combination of marketing and professional sales programs offered through the Michael J. Coles College of Business at Georgia's Kennesaw State University. Students can focus on any of the following career paths:

1. Professional selling. Students who follow this specialty concentrate on business-to-business selling. They acquire skills such as designing and delivering effective sales presentations, analyzing and managing individual accounts and markets, developing sales plans, and managing the sales force.
2. Promotional communications. In this area, students focus on the workings of the direct-marketing industry, advertising, and public relations. Although this concentration prepares students for a wide variety of careers, many of the skills covered can apply to sales and marketing in technical areas. The track emphasizes activities such as developing and targeting direct mailings, managing advertising functions, and selecting media.
3. Retail management. Students who concentrate in this area learn to assess competitive retail markets, analyze trading areas and site locations, determine procurement and inventory-control strategies, and manage and control merchandise. Most of those who pursue this concentration enter retail executive-training programs or take retail-management positions. Some follow retail-buying careers.
4. General marketing. Students who choose the general marketing area may select courses appropriate to career goals. Typically, this involves choosing from courses in sales, retailing, promotion, international marketing, sports marketing, and services marketing.

In the area of marketing, students may pursue a major in marketing while completing a bachelor's in business administration. This consists of general education requirements of forty-five credit hours including economics and specified math courses, a lower-division business core, upper-division major requirements, and a selection of business and nonbusiness electives.

The lower-division core includes the following courses:

Introduction to Financial Accounting
Introduction to Managerial Accounting
Principles of Microeconomics (counted in general education)
Principles of Macroeconomics
Business Information Systems and Communications
Legal & Ethical Environment of Business

Upper-division major requirements include the following:

Business Statistics
Principles of Finance
Principles of Marketing
Management & Behavioral Science
Operations Management
Strategic Management
Information Technology Management
Marketing Research
Consumer Behavior
International Marketing
Marketing Management

In addition, students select twelve credit hours from the following:

Basic Retailing
Retail Merchandise Management & Control
Retail Management
Professional Selling
Market Analysis
Sales Management
Services Marketing

Direct Response Marketing
Advertising
Promotional Strategy
Business to Business Marketing
Sports Marketing
Special Topics in Marketing

For more information contact:

Kennesaw State University
1000 Chastain Road
Kennesaw, GA 30144

Northern Illinois University

The College of Business at Northern Illinois University, through its Department of Marketing, offers a comprehensive sales-track curriculum. It helps prepare students for entry-level sales positions as well as career advancement. Students who pursue this track complete three sales-specific courses in addition to a general marketing curriculum. Courses include:

Principles of selling: Covers basic concepts, principles, and techniques for selling including analyzing customers, opening sales, ensuring effective communications, handling objections, closing sales, and improving customer satisfaction.

Sales management: Covers responsibilities and functions of sales managers including evaluating sales organizational structures; recruiting, selecting, testing, and training of salespeople; and managing compensation plans, control of expenses, sales forecasting, routing, quotas, questions of ethics, and motivation activities.

Advanced professional selling: Focuses on relationship and consultative selling with emphasis on value-added selling, major-account selling, coordination between salespeople and the firm's other functional areas, team selling, negotiating, communication styles, career management, and personal development.

Northern Illinois also offers two graduate-level courses in this area through its M.B.A. curriculum, Personal Selling for Managers and Sales Administration. More information is available from:

Northern Illinois University
De Kalb, IL 60115

Humber College

Toronto's Humber College offers an unusual program for college graduates who desire to broaden an academic background with a skill-based program in marketing management. It helps students develop skills in areas such as communications, interpersonal skills, customer service, creative problem solving, research, decision making, advertising and promotion, professional selling, and marketing strategies.

The program, which may be applied toward master's degree study at graduate institutions, consists of two semesters of study. Case studies, simulations, and research projects are utilized to provide students with experience in facing challenges commonly found in the marketing world. During the first semester, the following courses are completed:

Fundamentals of Marketing
Marketing Leadership
Professional Selling
International Trade

Second semester courses include:

Research for Marketing Management
Distribution
Advertising, Sales Promotion, and Public Relations
Marketing Management
Marketing Seminar

Graduates of this program have obtained positions including marketing assistant, assistant manager, sales support, network representative, account executive, owner/manager, distribution supervisor, account supervisor, merchandise assistant manager, marketing coordinator, production coordinator, sales and marketing representative, and senior marketing executive.

For more information contact:

The Business School at Humber College
205 Humber College Boulevard
Toronto, ON M9W 5L7
Canada

University of Arizona

Listed below are some representative marketing courses offered by the University of Arizona. Arizona's programs are typical of offerings that focus on the broad area of marketing rather than the more specific topic of sales. Many students take marketing courses as a background for sales work, and most marketing programs include at least some courses focusing on sales.

Introduction to marketing: Addresses the role of marketing on the economy and on business and nonprofit organizations, on environmental factors affecting marketing, and on the nature of marketing management decisions.

Services marketing: Covers marketing concepts and techniques for organizations whose core product is service. Topics include quality service delivery, customer attraction and retention, relationship marketing, etc.

Marketing research: Covers concepts and techniques of research for marketing decisions, problem definition, determination of information needs, sources, methods of gathering and analyzing data, and presentation of findings for management.

Buyer behavior: Looks at customer behavior and the application of concepts and research findings from the behavioral sciences in the solution of marketing problems.

Advertising and promotional management: Addresses the role of advertising and special promotions in the economy and business and nonprofit organizations, concepts and strategy for programs, budgets, media selection, and evaluation of effectiveness.

Management of sales operations: Covers the sales function and its relationship to the total marketing program, sales strategies and objectives, development and administration of sales organizations, and control and evaluation of sales operations.

Management of distribution systems: Focuses on the nature and operation of channels in the distribution of goods and services, economic and behavioral problems in wholesaling and retailing, and marketing logistics.

International marketing management: Studies the marketing operations for foreign environments and the cultural, political, and economic factors affecting the international marketer.

Product management: Focuses on product (services) strategies for achieving financial growth, evaluating opportunities, generating ideas, launching new offerings, and managing the product (services) portfolio.

Marketing policies and operations: This is an integrative, capstone course focusing on comprehensive marketing problems and the development, control, and auditing of marketing organizations and operations.

Marketing research for entrepreneurs: Discusses concepts and techniques of research for marketing decisions with a focus on new ventures and new product development.

Marketing management: Looks at the scope, environment, and nature of marketing management as well as customer and market analysis for product, service, price, promotion, and distribution decisions.

Business communication in marketing: This covers one unit of a three-course module designed to improve the oral and written communication skills of M.B.A. students preparing for business leadership careers. In this module, students learn to prepare and deliver oral presentations and written documents that focus on effective communication in the business discipline of marketing.

Management of marketing communications: Applies communications theory and research findings in advertising, sales promotion, publicity, and personal selling; and in the planning, conduct, and administration of programs of information and persuasion.

Consumer and organizational buyer behavior: Studies the nature of the purchase decision process for goods and services.

Theories, concepts, and research methods and findings are examined for use in management and public policy decision making.

Industrial marketing: Addresses problems and methods of marketing decision-making in industrial, government, and high-tech markets.

Product strategy: Focuses on formulating and implementing strategies for growth; analyzing and influencing market structure; developing, pricing, and testing new entries; and managing the portfolio.

International marketing: Covers marketing planning and strategies for foreign environments and the cultural, political, and economic factors affecting the international marketer, multinational corporation, and multinational market groups.

Environmental scanning and business strategy: An M.B.A. integrative course. Discusses how information from the economy can be used to develop a firm's competitive strategy. Is multidisciplinary in nature, using concepts from economics, marketing, and management. Includes case method approach to problems facing top management in making and effecting a strategic plan.

Marketing research for managers: Covers specification of management information needs, evaluation of research proposals and findings, methods of gathering and analyzing data, and administrative aspects of research and decisions.

Survey and qualitative marketing research methods: Focuses on survey and qualitative research for marketing management information needs; secondary data search methods; instrumentation, sampling, fieldwork, and data analysis; and ethnographic, depth interview, and projective methods.

Experimental research methods in marketing: Covers statistical, methodological, and interpretive issues in the design of laboratory and field experiments/quasi-experiments for marketing and consumer research.

For more information about marketing courses, degree programs, and related matters, contact:

Department of Marketing
The University of Arizona
P.O. Box 210108
Tucson, AZ 85721-0108

Southern Methodist University

An interesting option that does not involve completing an entire graduate degree is a certificate program offered by the Cox School of Business at Southern Methodist University. This Graduate Marketing Certificate helps students sharpen marketing competency and skills.

Designed primarily for executives, the program utilizes a variety of instructional methods including supplemental text readings, special discussion groups, break-out sessions, case studies, business simulations, and guest lecturers.

The program is divided into three trimesters covering a period of about six weeks each. Typical topics of study include:

Targeting, Segmentation, and Positioning
Marketing and Selling Value
New Product and Services Development

Branding and Loyalty on the Internet
Database Marketing
Developing a Winning Marketing Plan

For more information about the program contact:

Cox School of Business
Southern Methodist University
Dallas, TX 75275

Fluno Center for Executive Education

The Management Institute of the Fluno Center for Executive Education offers more than one hundred different professional development seminars including a number of sessions related to sales and marketing. It also develops customized training programs.

Offerings include seminars on sales management, direct selling skills, and customer service, among other topics. Of particular interest to those new to the profession is a program providing intensive training for new sales staff. It covers a wide range of selling fundamentals including pre-call planning and customer-oriented selling skills.

More details are available from:

Fluno Center for Executive Education
601 University Avenue
Madison, WI 53715

Ball State University

The Professional Selling Institute at Ball State University sponsors a number of activities related to sales careers, including conducting training for employed sales personnel and offering sales courses and opportunities for students.

The Professional Selling Institute designs and conducts innovative research and offers training and service activities. The latter includes both state-of-the-art training for practicing salespeople and advanced sales courses offered within the university's business curriculum.

Courses are offered in professional selling, advanced professional selling, and sales management. In addition, students assist with outside sales projects for actual companies.

Additional information is available from:

Ball State University
Muncie, IN 47306

University of Akron

The Ronald R. and Diane C. Fisher Institute for Professional Selling is part of the University of Akron's College of Business Administration. The institute enhances the image of the sales profession, promotes professional selling and sales management as rewarding lifelong careers, and offers education and training opportunities.

Its programs include a sales management major, a sales management minor, and a certificate in professional selling. The certificate program provides students with an opportunity to develop and document professional selling skills. It serves students from different backgrounds, including those with an interest in technical sales careers upon graduation. Customized sales training courses designed for corporate customers and public seminars on sales topics also are provided.

For more details contact:

Fisher Institute for Professional Selling
University of Akron
259 South Broadway Street, Suite 310
Akron, OH 44325-4804

Auburn University–Montgomery

The Sales and Marketing Director Certificate Program offered at Auburn University's campus in Montgomery, Alabama, helps sales professionals prepare for or build on experience in management positions.

The program focuses on strengthening selling skills, improving capabilities for managing other personnel, and building strong working skills with other employees and customers.

Courses offered in this certificate program include:

Professional Selling
Prospecting: The Key Ingredient
Negotiation
Effective Sales Management
Winning Presentations
Network Marketing and Publicity Power

For more details contact the university at:

Auburn University–Montgomery
Montgomery, AL 36117

Baylor University

Texas's Baylor University offers a number of courses covering sales principles including the following:

Professional selling and communications: A major focus of this course is the process of making informative and persuasive verbal presentations. Topics include product and service knowledge, prospecting, approach strategies, presentation materials and formats, handling customer questions and objections, reaching decisions, and servicing customers. Instructional strategies include case studies, role playing, group interaction, and use of professional speakers.

Sales force management and leadership: Common problems confronting first-line and second-line sales managers are examined in this course. Topics of study include employee recruiting, training, performance evaluation and feedback, compensation, goal setting, leadership, supervision, and coaching. A case-study format is utilized.

Professional selling and communications II: This course provides an in-depth study of advanced selling concepts such as relationships management, negotiation, the use of technology to enhance selling efficiency and effectiveness, and national account management.

Business to business marketing: The emphasis of this course is on marketing by firms to organizations rather than to households. The course stresses negotiation strategies along with management of relationships, purchasing, distribution channels, and distribution logistics.

You can obtain more information from:

College of Business
Baylor University
Waco, TX 76706

University of Florida

The College of Engineering at the University of Florida offers a program in sales engineering as an alternative to preparation for traditional engineering careers. Designed for engineering students only, this certificate program helps students acquire skills necessary for communicating effectively with other professionals while promoting and marketing new technologies and related products.

Courses that may be taken in pursuit of this certificate (some of which are required and some of which are electives from which students may choose) include:

Strategic Selling and the Technical Interface in Agribusiness
Technical Writing
Principles of Management
The Legal Environment of Business
Agricultural and Food Marketing
Engineering Economy
Civil Engineering Cost Analysis

For more information contact:

University of Florida College of Engineering
Office of Academic Programs
P.O. Box 116550
Gainesville, FL 32611-6550

Madonna University

The sales specialist certificate program offered by Madonna University provides relevant preparation for those already employed in the sales field as well as those who aspire to a career in sales. It is a nine-credit hour program integrating the study of marketing and use of selling strategies, with a focus on customer service.

The program's five courses are as follows:

Promotional Mix: Professional Selling
Promotional Mix: Theory and Practice of Teleselling
Promotional Mix: Sales Communication Strategies
Promotional Mix: Customer Service for Sales
Principles of Marketing

For more details contact:

Madonna University
36600 Schoolcraft
Livonia, MI 48150-1173

Ohio University

The Sales Centre at Ohio University promotes entrepreneurial thinking, sales excellence, and professionalism. Among its offerings is a creative sales certificate program, consisting of a twenty-eight-credit-hour cross-disciplinary undergraduate sales curriculum. An innovative feature of this program is that it requires a three-hundred-hour supervised, formal sales internship.

Students who complete the certificate program take the following courses:

Professional Selling
Sales Internship

Two advanced courses selected from:

Business to Business Marketing
Advanced Topics in Sales (sales management)
Current Topics in Sales: Executive in Residence

A communication requirement selected from:

Argumentative Analysis and Advocacy
Communication in Interpersonal Relationships

Two additional cross-disciplinary requirements selected from choices such as:

Engineering and Technology Overview
Introduction to Manufacturing

Introduction to Ethics
Acting Fundamentals I
The Theater Experience

The centre also promotes the sales profession by serving as an information clearinghouse and contact point for educators, sales professionals, relevant organizations, and the business community. It also fosters sales research and offers professional development and continuing education opportunities.

For more information contact:

The Sales Centre
Ohio University
Copeland Hall
Athens, OH 45701-2979

University of British Columbia

The University of British Columbia offers a diploma course in marketing and sales management. This is a three-year, university-level program designed to develop professional sales and marketing managers.

During the first year of the program, students concentrate on marketing and customer relationship management. During the second year, the focus is on marketing research, sampling, data collection, and data analysis, along with financial management topics such as an overview of financial statements, the assessment of financial performance, financial planning, sales forecasting, and capital budgeting. In the third year, the program presents the development of an integrated marketing framework and its applications to marketing strategy, taking the viewpoint of the marketing manager.

For application information and other details, contact:

University of British Columbia
Marketing and Sales Management Diploma Program
1500 West Georgia Street
Vancouver, BC V6G 2Z6
Canada

TWO-YEAR COLLEGE PROGRAMS

A practical option for preparing for a sales career is to attend a community college and pursue a two-year associate degree or a one-year certificate program in marketing or a related area (or to complete a program of this duration offered by a four-year college). Obviously, completion of such a program will not qualify one for a position requiring a bachelor's degree, but many positions are available that do not require a bachelor's degree, especially entry-level jobs.

In addition, various options can be followed while pursuing a two-year degree or following its completion. Possible options include completing a technical program (or selected technical courses) in conjunction with the marketing program to gain technical competencies. For example, a two-year marketing degree might be enhanced with courses in areas such as computing, electronics, drafting, or other areas. Another possibility is to enter the sales workforce once you've obtained your degree and advance through positive job experience. Or you could transfer to a four-year college immediately following completion of an associate degree or pursue a four-year degree on a part-time basis while working as a sales professional, perhaps with financial support from the employer.

Following are descriptions of college-level sales programs that may be completed in two or fewer years.

Kingwood College

For those interested in sales or marketing careers, the associate degree program offered by Kingwood College in Texas is typical of programs offered by community, junior, and technical colleges.

Following is a representative sequence of courses in this area:

First Semester
Introduction to Management
Composition and Rhetoric I
approved elective
Sales Strategies and Tactics
Computer Keyboarding (or computer elective)

Second Semester
Sales Management
Retail Operations and Methodology
Marketing Management
Math/Natural Science
Public Speaking (or related course)
Business Speech
Physical Activity

Third Semester
Organizational Theory and Human Behavior
Marketing Promotion and Advertising
Marketing Co-op Work Experience and Seminar I
Microeconomics or Macroeconomics
Principles of Accounting I

Fourth Semester
Management Development
Marketing Co-op Work Experience and Seminar II

Marketing Research
elective in the humanities or fine arts
elective in an outside area of specialization

For more details contact:

Kingwood College
20000 Kingwood Drive
Kingwood, TX 77339

Joliet Junior College

Through its Sales and Marketing Institute, Joliet Junior College in Illinois offers a Certificate in Sales and Marketing (CSM), which recognizes the professional competency of sales and marketing executives who have met high standards of education, experience, and knowledge. This certificate also recognizes knowledge, leadership, and professionalism in sales personnel.

To become certified, participants must accumulate a specified number of points designating various professional qualifications, obtain professional references verifying experience and competency, and submit an application.

Qualifying points are awarded based on formal education, experience as a full-time sales representative or full-time sales/marketing manager, and continuing sales and marketing education.

For more information contact:

Joliet Junior College
Sales and Marketing Institute
214 North Ottawa Street
Joliet, IL 60432

New York University

The Paul McGhee undergraduate degree program for adults at New York University provides students with the opportunity to complete an associate degree program in marketing. As pointed out by the university, the field of marketing covers a number of diverse functions including sales, advertising, public relations, product management, and marketing research. In this program, students fulfill a core requirement of twenty-eight credits.

They also meet an eight-credit professional studies requirement in marketing principles and complete sixteen credits from among the following courses:

Business Law
Internship in Business and Organizational Behavior
Database Design
Multimedia Presentations
Algebra and Calculus with Applications to Business and
    Economics
Organizational Behavior

For more details contact:

New York University
School of Continuing and Professional Studies
New York, NY 10012

ASSOCIATION-SPONSORED TRAINING

Professional organizations also provide a variety of training opportunities. For example, the Manufacturers Representatives Educational Research Foundation (MRERF) has programs designed to foster personal, professional, and organizational growth. The foundation's educational subsidiary, the Institute for Professional Advancement, provides educational opportunities such as a certification program for owners, managers, or heirs of representative, broker, and agency firms; Multiple Lines Sales Training for salespeople within a firm (designed primarily for those new to the multiple-lines sales function or those who have had five or fewer years of experience); continuing education programs for graduates of the certification program; and a self-paced course, "Synergistic Selling for the Twenty-First Century."

For other opportunities, see the information provided by specific associations in which you are interested. Chapter 8 provides more details on professional associations.

PRIVATE TRAINING FIRMS

Some training opportunities are offered by companies specializing in training, consulting, or other business and professional services rather than by colleges, universities, or nonprofit institutions. Following are two examples.

Sales Training International

A good example of a private training firm is Sales Training International. This is a sales, sales management, and customer service training company that also offers consulting and product development services. It provides sales training courses as well as training in sales management, customer service, and other areas. Examples of training topics include sales process coordination, marketing support, customer satisfaction, and communications infrastructure. Typical courses include a Sales Professionals Academy, ACE Teleselling, Principled Negotiations, Time and

Territory Management, Goal Setting, and a Competitor Analysis Strategy Session.

For more information contact the company at the following address:

Sales Training International
2204 Timberloch Place, Suite 150
The Woodlands, TX 77380

Sales Concepts

This company, which was established in 1981, provides customized training programs. It utilizes various formats including sales meetings, customized courses, continuing training programs, train-the-trainer programs, and other types of training activities.

For more information contact:

Sales Concepts
610 Hembree Parkway, Suite 407
Roswell, GA 30076

COMPANY TRAINING PROGRAMS

Many employers offer company training for beginning sales personnel. Some programs may last up to two years, but programs of shorter duration are becoming increasingly common. Such programs can be a good way for the inexperienced to get started in sales work. They also may prove beneficial for more experienced workers who need to become oriented to a new company or an area in which they have not previously worked.

For more information about company training programs, check with any potential employer in which you are interested.

CHAPTER 8

PROFESSIONAL ASSOCIATIONS

In most career areas, including sales, interacting with people holding similar responsibilities is an integral component of job success. Sales professionals, as well as students and others who would like to pursue a sales or marketing career, can benefit in a number of ways by associating with others who share common interests. Some of the best vehicles for building and maintaining such relationships are professional associations.

Professional associations vary in size and scope. Some are national or international, while others serve regional or local memberships. In many cases, a combination of the two is offered, with members of national groups also participating in state or local chapters of the parent organization.

The membership of most associations consists of voluntary members who share common interests. Typically, officers are selected from within the membership. Many such groups also have executive directors and other staff who are paid to coordinate the association's day-to-day activities.

BENEFITS OF PARTICIPATING IN
PROFESSIONAL ASSOCIATIONS

Many sales personnel find it beneficial to participate in professional associations. The benefits vary among groups and individuals, but they may include the following:

- the chance to network with other sales professionals who face similar job challenges
- the opportunity to learn from more experienced sales pros or those with expertise in specific areas
- the opportunity to participate in conferences, training sessions, or other activities sponsored by the association
- the chance to keep up with new developments through newsletters, magazines, websites, or other means of communication
- the potential to benefit from services and programs such as government relations efforts, group insurance, or discounts on products or services related to the profession
- the opportunity to take advantage of the image of professionalism fostered by professional associations, including an emphasis on ethical sales practices
- the potential to identify sales job openings

REPRESENTATIVE ASSOCIATIONS

Following is an overview of a number of associations. Some focus on the needs of technical sales professionals or the interests of specific technical fields, while others serve the needs of sales personnel from both technical and nontechnical areas.

Canadian Office Products Association

The Canadian Office Products Association represents the interests of the office products industry. Formed in 1933, it changed its name to the current usage in 1968. The organization provides industry-related information for members, holds professional conferences, provides continuing education opportunities, sponsors publications, and provides other services.

For more information contact:

Canadian Office Products Association
4920 de Maisonneuve, Suite 305
Westmount, Quebec H3Z 1N1
Canada

Canadian Professional Sales Association

In operation since 1874, the Canadian Professional Sales Association helps sales professionals sharpen skills and advance their careers. It serves more than thirty thousand members. The association provides training opportunities, networking, information services, publications, and other services. Of special interest is a program leading to a Certified Sales Professional designation.

More details are available from:

Canadian Professional Sales Association
145 Wellington Street West, Suite 610
Toronto, ON M5J 1H8
Canada

Customer Relationship Management Association

The Customer Relationship Management Association (CRMA) of Canada is a nonprofit organization serving Canadian executives and businesses. It focuses on transferring independent knowledge about customer relations management and setting standards for the practice of successful CRM.

The association provides educational courses aimed at the management level, networking opportunities, a resource directory, and other services.

More information about the organization is available from:

CRMA Canada
411 Richmond Street East
Toronto, ON M5A 3S5
Canada

Direct Selling Association

The Direct Selling Association (DSA) is a national trade association of leading firms that manufacture and distribute goods and services sold directly to consumers. According to the association, this type of sale consists of "the sale of a consumer product or service in a face to face manner away from a fixed retail location."

The DSA promotes ethical business practices and consumer service through its code of ethics. The organization's membership is composed of national direct selling associations in more than fifty countries.

More details are available from:

Direct Selling Association
1275 Pennsylvania Avenue NW, Suite 800
Washington, DC 20004

Electrical Equipment Representatives Association

The Electrical Equipment Representatives Association (EERA) provides a forum for industry representatives to discuss matters pertinent to their professional success and the interests of the industry. The association promotes standards of excellence, fosters communication and cooperation, and studies and disseminates information about efficient business systems. The EERA also provides other services such as assisting in analysis of markets within specific territories, exchanging information on training and compensation of sales personnel, and communicating information about legislation related to the industry.

More information is available from:

Electrical Equipment Representatives Association
P.O. Box 419264
Kansas City, MO 64141-6264

Electro-Federation Canada

Electro-Federation Canada is an organization of about two hundred companies in the electrical, electronics, appliance, and telecommunications industries. It promotes dialogue on issues affecting the electro-technical businesses and promotes communication, including opportunities for members from the different segments of the industry to deal with issues specific to their sector.

The organization provides statistical market and business data, special reports and forecasts, and other business information. It also maintains relationships with other influential organizations throughout North America, influences government policy, and supports training and development.

For more details contact:

Electro-Federation Canada
5800 Explorer Drive, Suite 200
Mississauga, ON L4W 5K9
Canada

Electronics Representatives Association

The Electronics Representatives Association (ERA) consists of more than 1,300 professional manufacturers along with about 350 manufacturer members who out-source field sales to the association's members.

The organization provides a variety of educational and communications programs. It offers a directory of electronics representatives, supports special interest groups, promotes professional standards, and encourages members to follow a code of ethics, among other activities.

More information is available from:

Electronics Representatives Association
444 North Michigan Avenue, Suite 1960
Chicago, IL 60611

International Biometric Industry Association

Founded in 1998, the International Biometric Industry Association (IBIA) is a trade association that advances, advocates, defends, and supports the collective interests of the biometric industry.

Although not a sales organization, the IBIA is typical of trade organizations serving industries specializing in highly technical products. As such, it would be of interest to sales personnel in areas related to biometrics.

It provides a variety of services to members and serves as a clearinghouse on information about the biometrics industry.

For more information contact:

International Biometric Industry Association
601 Thirteenth Street NW, Suite 370 South
Washington, DC 20005

International Customer Service Association

Promoting development and awareness of the customer service profession through networking, education, and research is the main agenda of the International Customer Service Association (ICSA). Founded 1981 by a group of fifty-nine customer service management professionals, the association now boasts more than thirty-four hundred members.

Some of the industries represented by members include technical fields such as chemicals and allied products, medical and diagnostics products, and electrical and electronic equipment.

Services to members include an annual conference, the publication of surveys and member research studies, and promotional efforts on the behalf of the customer service profession.

For more details contact the organization at:

International Customer Service Association
401 North Michigan Avenue
Chicago, IL 60611

Manufacturers' Agents National Association

This professional organization serves professional manufacturers' agents while also offering associate membership for manufacturers and other interested parties. It offers a mechanism for sharing knowledge among experienced agents and manufacturers, representing members' interests at the state and national political levels, promoting business development in other countries, and meeting other goals.

Of special interest is an on-line database of manufacturers' sales agencies. Used by more than 50,000 marketing professionals to locate the country's top agencies, this helpful information source is updated on a weekly basis. It lists more than 5,200 agencies that represent 21,000 agents, and it can be searched by terms such as "territory," "agency," "location," "product classifi-cation," "customers served," and "services offered."

The association also publishes *Agency Sales Magazine* and a quarterly newsletter as well as offering contract guidelines, a state law manual, research bulletins, and special reports. It sponsors regional seminars, offers a counseling service and information exchange, and provides training and certification programs, among other benefits and services.

For more information contact:

Manufacturers' Agents National Association
23016 Mill Creek Drive
P.O. Box 3467
Laguna Hills, CA 92654-3467
www.manaonline.org

Manufacturers Representatives Educational Research Foundation

The Manufacturers Representatives Educational Research Foundation (MRERF) is a nonprofit entity providing efforts to enhance public awareness about the independent multiple-line selling organization. It provides professional education, supports research, and provides information on the value of the function to the marketplace.

The organization focuses on supporting professional education through certification and sales training, promoting academic study, and providing information to the business community.

For more information contact:

Manufacturers Representatives Educational Research Foundation
P.O. Box 247
Geneva, IL 60134

National Association of Sales Professionals

Certification is an important consideration with the National Association of Sales Professionals (NASP). Members can earn recognition as a Certified Professional Sales Person (CPSP). This generally indicates that a member is a top achiever who typically ranks in the upper 10 percent of his or her field or company in terms of sales performance.

A major purpose of this organization is to link certified, career-minded salespeople together into a global network. All persons accepted for membership are enrolled in the International Registry of Accredited Salespersons.

For more information contact:

National Association of Sales Professionals
8300 North Hayden Road, Suite 207
Scottsdale, AZ 85258

National Electrical Manufacturers Representatives Association

The National Electrical Manufacturers Representatives Association (NEMRA) promotes the use of independent manufacturers' representatives in marketing electrical products. It serves as a resource for electrical manufacturers to access more than sixty-five hundred salespeople who call on all facets of the electrical industry. The organization also provides members with education, training, group services, and networking opportunities.

The association provides a wide variety of programs and services for members, including publications, member identification and recognition, and support in areas such as insurance, legal matters, and scholarships.

For more details contact:

National Electrical Manufacturers Representatives Association
660 White Plains Road, Suite 600
Tarrytown, NY 10591

North American Industrial Representatives Association

The North American Industrial Representatives Association
(NIRA) serves manufacturers' representatives of industrial products. It fosters respect for the industry, promotes the advantages of
doing business through manufacturers' representatives, and provides a variety of benefits and services to members.

For more information contact:

North American Industrial Representatives Association
175 North Harbor Drive, Suite 1205
Chicago, IL 60601

Power-Motion Technology Representatives Association

This organization has served representatives in the power transmission and motion control industries, and their manufacturer
principals, since 1972. The PTRA supports the work of
manufacturers' "reps" by providing a variety of professional services, conferences, and educational opportunities. It promotes the
development of Web-based marketing services and provides discounts on group insurance and long-distance telephone services,
among other activities for members.

For more information contact:

Power-Motion Technology Representatives Association
330 South Wells Street, Suite 1422
Chicago, IL 60606

Safety Equipment Manufacturers Agents Association

Operating as a not-for-profit association, the Safety Equipment Manufacturers Agents Association (SEMAA) promotes the function and professionalism of industrial products representatives both individually and as a group.

It works to foster a spirit of mutual respect and esteem among members, provides educational programs, and promotes the multiple-line representative function. It provides a variety of benefits and services to its members.

More details may be obtained by contacting the organization at the following address:

Safety Equipment Manufacturers Agents Association
175 North Harbor Drive, Suite 1205
Chicago, IL 60601

Sales Association of the Chemical Industry

Formed in 1921, the Sales Association of the Chemical Industry serves members representing more than 350 companies in the chemical industry and related areas. A major goal of the association is increasing the efficiency of the sales process. It fosters high ethical standards, encourages networking among chemical sales professionals as well as those involved in purchasing or promotion, and promotes positive recognition for the chemical marketing profession.

Services to members include professional networking opportunities, sales and educational seminars, professional meetings, fellowship events, and publications.

For additional information contact:

Sales Association of the Chemical Industry
66 Morris Avenue, Suite 2A
Springfield, NJ 07081

Sales & Marketing Executives – International

This organization traces its origins to the nineteenth century, when sales managers' clubs were formed to improve the image and public standing of sales professionals. The organization now known as SME got its start in 1935, when a group calling itself the National Federation of Sales Executives was formed. It changed its name to National Sales Executives (NSE) International in 1949, and then became Sales & Marketing Executives (SME) – International in the 1960s.

Members of this organization include chief executive officers, marketing executives, sales managers, and business owners. The organization provides a number of benefits for members including publications, a daily "Sales and Marketing Breaking News" E-mail report, an on-line library on sales and marketing, and various professional meetings.

For more details contact:

Sales & Marketing Executives – International
P.O. Box 1390
Sumas, WA 98295-1390

Strategic Account Management Association

This organization maintains a comprehensive network of practitioners, researchers, academics, and consultants who are interested in customer-supplier partnering. It supports the professional and personal development of executives who manage national, global, and strategic account relationships.

The association publishes a quarterly magazine, *Velocity,* and offers an extensive on-line library of white papers, research briefs, case studies, and other types of information. It also sponsors courses and seminars, fosters peer networking, and maintains special interest groups.

More information is available by contacting:

Strategic Account Management Association
150 North Wacker Drive, Suite 2222
Chicago, IL 60606

CHAPTER 9

SALARIES AND BENEFITS

Just how much money can one expect to make in this field? That is an important consideration, and in the case of sales, a key motivation for many sales practitioners.

Salaries earned by technical sales professionals vary widely. In a store-based retail job, earnings may be much lower than in a high-level position involving business-to-business sales of high-cost products or services. In many cases earnings may be excellent, especially in situations where commissions or bonuses are awarded to successful sales work.

METHOD OF PAYMENT

Salaries and wages earned by technical sales professionals vary not only in the amount of money earned but in the way in which payment is determined. In some cases, employees are paid salaries calculated on a weekly, monthly, or yearly basis. In others, their pay is made up entirely of commissions calculated as a percentage of sales they attain. A combination of the two is a common approach.

The practice of basing income on sales distinguishes this field from many others. Not surprisingly, this approach offers both advantages and disadvantages. On the negative side, there can be a lack of stability in income. On the positive side, the practice of earning commissions allows those who perform exceptionally well to be paid accordingly.

FACTORS AFFECTING EARNINGS

In the sales world, a number of factors come into play in determining earnings. Of course, for those who work on a commission basis, the three main factors are the prices of products, the volume of sales, and the commission rate, with the latter tending to reflect the normal practices followed within any industry.

Other considerations that may help determine salary levels include educational background, previous job experience, geographic location, size and type of employer, level of responsibility, previous salary levels, and competition for employees skilled in technical sales.

AVERAGE EARNINGS

According to the U.S. Department of Labor, the median annual earnings of sales representatives outside of the retail area were more than $36,500 in 1998, including commissions. This meant that half of all sales professionals earned more than this amount, and half earned less. The middle 50 percent earned between $26,350 and $51,580 yearly. Some earned less, and others earned substantially more.

Median salaries for sales representatives in specific technology-based industries included the following:

electrical goods	$36,700
machinery, equipment, and supplies	$36,400
professional and commercial equipment	$35,300

Sales engineers earned median salaries (including commissions) of $54,000 in 1998. The middle 50 percent earned from $41,240 to $79,480. Median earnings for sales engineers in specific industries were:

computer and data processing services	$62,800
electrical goods	$56,600
machinery, equipment, and supplies	$48,900
professional and commercial equipment	$51,700

Sales personnel who work as manufacturers' agents do not earn salaries or wages. Instead, they are paid on a commission basis, which normally is calculated as a percentage of the sales amount for a given purchase. For successful sales agents, earning potential can be excellent. At the same time, those who function under this type of arrangement also must pay their own expenses.

Earnings in other sales areas vary widely. Beginners in retail sales may earn very low wages, while senior pros in high-tech fields may pull down six-figure incomes.

BENEFITS

In addition to salaries, wages, commissions, or bonuses, many employers offer liberal fringe benefits. Benefits vary a great deal, with some employers offering a bare minimum and others providing a broad-based benefits program. Benefits may include some or all of the following:

stock options or other profit sharing
paid vacations
holidays
sick time or related time off (such as maternity leave)
personal time
retirement plans

medical insurance
dental insurance
life insurance
travel or accident insurance
disability insurance
retiree benefits
tuition assistance
death benefits

Sales professionals also may earn other types of benefits or "perks" such as frequent flier mileage, mileage reimbursement, or use of a company car, in some cases including personal as well as professional use. They may earn incentives such as bonuses, free vacation trips, or prizes for outstanding sales performance.

CHAPTER 10

GETTING STARTED

There are a number of different approaches to pursuing a career in technical sales. Once the necessary credentials have been established through education or other means, the first step in pursuing a sales career is to identify job openings. This can be done in any number of ways. For college students, a good starting point is your school's career services or job placement office. Such an office typically will provide job listings, resume assistance, and other services, and it also may hold job fairs or sponsor other opportunities to meet with potential employers. For high school students, the careers services office of a local college may serve potential students or the public at large.

USING THE INTERNET

When seeking jobs, an increasingly valuable resource is the Internet. One of the pluses of the Internet age is that much more information about employers is available than ever before. Such information can be useful not only in identifying job openings, but also in learning about potential employers and their backgrounds.

For example, say you'd like to learn more about corporate giant IBM so that you can be better informed when inquiring about job openings or applying for available positions. If you simply key in the company's easily identifiable URL, www.ibm.com, you'll access its corporate website.

Among the choices you'll find is the heading of "Jobs at IBM." If you click on that, you'll go to a Web page that provides additional employment-related information, including the fact that IBM employs more than three hundred thousand people worldwide, along with a list containing the following areas in which jobs may be found: the United States, Canada, Latin America, Europe, Africa, the Middle East, and the Asia-Pacific region. Once a region of preference is selected, you can choose from headings such as "Find a Job," "Submit Resume," or "Working at IBM." If you select "Find a Job," you can search from corporation-wide job openings by using a keyword such as "sales."

But that's not the whole story. In addition to information related directly to job openings, most corporate websites also provide a wealth of detail about the company itself. Reading through this kind of information can be helpful in a number of ways. Most important, it can help familiarize you with facts that could be useful in the job application and interview process, since the greater your understanding of the company, the better you can focus your comments during interviews, phone conversations, or correspondence with company officials. Such information also can be useful in helping you decide right away if a given company is sufficiently appealing for you to continue to explore it as a possible employer.

At IBM's main site, you can choose from an expansive menu of choices. This includes a corporate history, overviews of community relations and governmental relations programs, a look at the company's environmental philosophy, and details about current research efforts. You also can review financial information including the corporation's revenue, net income, and total assets.

In addition, you can peruse a full-fledged annual report covering the company's recent operations.

Other companies' websites offer similar information. Taking the time to review such details can be an important step in the job search process.

Also, don't overlook the potential offered by Internet-based job placement services. In recent years, a number of on-line services that assist job hunters or help prospective employers identify new personnel have emerged. These sites offer some real advantages. Many are free, with employers or advertisers footing the bill. They also are easily accessed, current, and in many cases highly informative.

An example is career.com. It provides key information for bringing companies and job seekers together with a minimum of hassles. Launched in 1993, the company advertises that it was the first "dot-com" recruitment advertising service. It offers a number of innovations including interactive recruiting, a "Hot Jobs" feature for showcasing critical jobs, virtual job fairs, and a private resume database. For more details, check out this site at www.career.com.

Other examples include hotjobs.com and monster.com, which provide details on jobs in all kinds of employment areas, and sales.com, which focuses more on sales. Other such services can be identified simply by keying in phrases such as "job" or "sales jobs" using any Internet search engine.

TRADITIONAL APPROACHES

A more traditional but still valid practice is consulting the classified sections of newspapers and reviewing ads placed by companies seeking sales personnel. Newspapers published in smaller cities will include ads for local job openings. For regional or national openings, you'll need to look at major papers such as the *Washington Post* or *New York Times*.

Publications provided by professional associations and employment newsletters also may be consulted for job listings.

Of course, you can always contact companies directly and request information on job openings and how you might apply. A call or letter to the human resources office can get you started. So can a look at a potential employer's site on the World Wide Web. Almost all of the major companies now maintain an on-line presence, and more and more smaller firms also are providing information on-line.

Other sources of job information include publications targeted specifically to those who are already employed in sales or in management positions and those related to the sales and marketing function.

GETTING AN INSIDE LOOK

Before making any type of commitment toward a career in this area, a smart move is to gather firsthand information about what working in sales is really like. In the process, you can assess how likely it is that your own interests, abilities, and overall goals will mesh with the realities of such a job. Consider some of the following steps while you're still in school or before you actually begin pursuing full-time employment in a sales or related area.

- There is nothing like real-life experience to help you in making career-related decisions. Consider taking a part-time or summer job in retail sales or another sales area to gain some valuable exposure to the sales world. One advantage of retail sales, especially in stores employing large numbers of workers, is that employee turnover levels are frequently high. This means that new positions open up all the time, especially for part-time workers. Similarly, some companies actively seek college students for summer sales assignments. By taking on a part-time or summer job, you can get a firsthand look at the many aspects of a sales position. Of course, this will apply only to entry-level positions, but you also can observe more experienced workers and gain an idea of what their work involves. In searching for summer employment opportunities, a good source of information is the AboutJobs.com network. It offers a website geared toward those seeking summer jobs (www.SummerJobs.com). The site provides tips on topics such as resumes, work permits, career-related reading, and other relevant matters. It also includes a searchable database of summer employment opportunities around the nation as well as in other countries.

- Complete an internship in sales or marketing. An internship can provide many of the advantages of part-time or summer employment, while also helping to meet academic requirements if you are a business major or are studying in a related area. In addition, most employers offering internship programs also make a special effort to see that the experience is an enlightening one.

   Some internships consist of paid positions maintained on a temporary basis. In many cases they are set up so you can earn college credit while also developing important job skills. In the area of sales, they might allow you to focus on such matters as acquiring technical competencies, customer service experience, and development of various professional sales skills. In addition, they can provide a firsthand look at your future career choice while providing financial compensation.

   Some internships offer the same basic advantages but on an unpaid basis. These are less common in the world of sales, however, than in many other areas, such as putting in time with nonprofit organizations.

A helpful source of information about internships is the previously mentioned AboutJobs.com network, which maintains a website dedicated specifically to internship opportunities (www.internjobs.com). This site provides a searchable database of available internships. A recent search using the keyword "sales" resulted in a list of thirty-six available internships in various areas of sales. A number of these were in technical fields. Although the number of internships varies at any given time, the site remains a good source of information throughout the year for those interested in checking out internship possibilities.

Each listing includes a job description and contact information for the sponsoring company. The site also provides other resources including links to sites focusing on permanent job opportunities.

- Enroll in sales classes or seminars. Chapter 7 provides a detailed look at typical programs and courses in sales, marketing, or related areas. College courses can provide an excellent introduction to many aspects of sales and sales management. Short-term classes and seminars also can be worthwhile, although many are designed as continuing education opportunities for those already employed in the field. In either case, the content covered not only will help prepare you for a potential sales career, but will provide you with the details you need to make informed occupational decisions.

- Take an interest inventory or a special type of exam designed to help you make career choices. You can find out more about such "exams" by contacting a guidance counselor, college career services office, or job-search company. Keep in mind that if you take an interest inventory you do not receive passing or failing scores. Instead, this process provides an analytical look at your interests based on information you provide in answering questions. The result can be a helpful part of the career planning process.

• Read more about sales and related areas. Books about sales are good sources of information, as are magazines targeted to sales professionals or members of professional associations.

For example, *Agency Sales Magazine,* offered by the Manufacturers' Agents National Association, is a good source of job information. Published monthly, the magazine covers important developments and issues on a national basis. Topics covered include tax developments and tips, market data, management aids, legal bulletins, and more. Most issues cover subjects such as government issues, industry news, tips on business development, commission surveys, marketing, and profiles of agents and manufacturers.

In addition to providing a wealth of information of interest to those employed as manufacturers agents, it also offers classified ads that include job openings in the field. Ads cover topics such as product lines wanted, manufacturers' agents wanted, and miscellaneous sales openings. The magazine can be accessed on-line at www.mana online.org.

Another publication worth checking out is *The Representor,* a magazine targeted to representatives and manufacturers in the electronics industry. Published by the Electronics Representatives Association, the magazine publishes news about the industry and other useful items. For subscription information or other details, contact:

Electronics Representatives Association
444 North Michigan Avenue, Suite 1960
Chicago, IL 60611

For those interested in sales opportunities in the pharmaceutical industry, a solid source of information is *Pharmaceutical Representative* magazine. This publication provides new product information along with recent drug approvals and industry news. It also offers updates on research breakthroughs, advice for improving selling skills, and continuing education information. Subscription information and other details are available at:

McKnight Medical Communications
Two Northfield Plaza, Suite 300
Northfield, IL 60093

See Appendix A for suggested further reading.

STRENGTHENING EMPLOYMENT POTENTIAL

As previously noted, job openings in sales and marketing have varying requirements. Some positions require previously developed technical knowledge. Others are suitable for those with a general knowledge of business principles. Some positions, especially those in sales management, require years of related job experience. Senior-level jobs would not be a realistic employment possibility for recent college graduates or other newcomers, but they can provide a goal for future attainment. Other jobs are designed as entry-level positions and provide an ideal way to get started in a sales career.

Regardless of the job level, most employers consider four basic factors in hiring new sales staff. The best job candidates will demonstrate strength in all four areas, although, of course, recent college graduates could not be expected to have attained extensive job experience. To enhance your own job prospects, do everything possible to demonstrate a positive record in the following areas:

1. *Education:* Obviously, holding a college degree with a directly related major is a key to many job openings. An engineering degree can lead to a position as a sales engineer, and a business or marketing major can provide the basis for a wide range of business positions, including those in sales. But although much emphasis is placed on the choice of a major, don't overlook the potential offered by individual courses. A student with an engineering degree who also took courses in marketing, for instance, might have an advantage over another job applicant who took engineering alone.

Even if you major in a liberal arts program or other nonbusiness field but complete a few courses related to sales and marketing, that can be a point in your favor if you apply for an entry-level sales position. If such courses do not fit into your program of study, perhaps you can take them as electives. One approach would be to complete sales- or marketing-related courses during the summer. Another possibility would be to attend a few noncredit seminars in this area.

It is important to realize that completing an entire degree may earn only a few lines on your resume. If you can list individual courses, seminars, or other sales-related learning experiences on a resume or job application, it can be a real plus in the job search.

2. *Job Experience:* As previously noted, many options exist for gaining work experience. Part-time employment, summer jobs, and internships all provide valuable work experience. Such experience will be useful not only in building appropriate knowledge but also for the simple but important factor of being able to cite it when applying for job openings.

As essential as being able to list job experience is an indication that you have done a good job. Experience alone is not sufficient if you have been ineffective or unreliable as an employee. For this reason, not to mention your own self-directed desire to succeed, a key ingredient in previous work experience is doing a good job. This will pay off when prospective employers contact those for whom you have previously been employed. As anyone in the business world will attest, positive job references will be invaluable in obtaining new positions.

3. *Related Skills:*   What if you do not yet have significant work experience? In this event, it may be difficult to demonstrate that you possess specific job-related skills that are appropriate for sales positions. Nevertheless, any success you have as a student should indicate that you have developed some important skills. In addition, job or volunteer experience can be used to enhance such capabilities.

For instance, if you have taken speech classes or other communications classes, acquired computing skills, or developed other skills that might be applied in a business setting, that will be to your advantage. The same is true if you have participated in a school-sponsored phonathon, held a student leadership position, or worked in a volunteer capacity for a nonprofit organization. Any skills in communicating, organizing, calculating, or computing may be cited as evidence of abilities that potentially might support sales-related work.

4. *Potential:*   Employers also may consider other indicators of potential. These can include factors such as: positive recommendations from teachers or professors; good grades; leadership positions or participation in business-related student organizations; student awards (such as academic awards, winning entries in speech contests or essay contests, etc.); ability to carry heavy workloads (such as working while attending school); volunteer experience; tangible evidence of skills mastered (for example, a Web page you've developed or samples of promotional materials you've written); traits such as a strong vocabulary, a good command of grammar and usage, and well-developed conversation

skills; and poise and personality as demonstrated in job interviews or social interaction.

Can you demonstrate strengths in any of these areas? If so, take advantage of them. In areas where you are weak, work on making improvements. With the right combination of education, experience, skills, and potential, you can position yourself to take advantage of position openings when they become available.

Keep in mind that getting started in sales is not all that different than starting out in other fields. Sooner or later you will need to acquire some specialized job skills, but it all starts out with a positive attitude and a willingness to work hard. After that, an old cliché holds that the sky is the limit. That may be a slight overstatement, but for the right person, a career in sales has much to offer.

FURTHER READING

Afeman, Lydia. *I Wanna Be a Sales Rep!: The Insider's Guide to Landing Great-Paying Jobs in Sales*. La Vergne, TN: Ingram Book Company, 1998.

Baggett, Byrd. *Satisfaction Guaranteed: 236 Ideas to Make Your Customers Feel Like a Million Dollars*. Nashville: Rutledge Hill Press, 1994.

Barnes, Myers. *Closing Strong: The Super Sales Handbook*. MBA Publications, 1997.

Camenson, Blythe and Jan Goldberg. *On the Job: Real People Working in Sales and Marketing*. Lincolnwood, IL: VGM Career Books, 1996.

Chitwood, Roy. *World Class Selling: The Complete Selling Process*. Best Seller's Publishing, 1996.

Crowel, Thomas Ray. *Simple Selling: Common Sense that Guarantees Your Success*. BookWorld Press, 1998.

Eberts, Marjorie and Margaret Gisler. *Careers for Talkative Types & Others with the Gift of Gab*. Lincolnwood, IL: VGM Career Books, 1998.

Ellis, Chad. *Opportunities in Medical Sales Careers*. Lincolnwood, IL: VGM Career Books, 1997.

Fox, Jeffrey. *How to Become a Rainmaker: The People Who Get and Keep Customers*. New York: Hyperion, 2000.

Futrell, Charles. *ABC's of Relationship Selling*. Burr Ridge, IL: Irwin Publishing, 1997.

Gross, T. Scott. *Outrageous!: Unforgettable Service...Guilt-Free Selling*. New York: American Management Association, 1998.

Hopkins, Tom. *Sales Closing for Dummies*. Foster City, CA: IDG Books, 1998.

Jolles, Robert L. *Customer Centered Selling: Eight Steps to Success from the World's Best Sales Force*. New York: The Free Press, 1998.

Kerzic, Nikki. *Medical & Pharmaceutical Sales: How to Land the Job of Your Dreams*. Brecksville, OH: Executive Connection, 1999.

Kline, Phil. *Make the Change to Customer-Driven Sales*. Amherst, MA: HRD Press, 1997.

Kossen, Stan. *Careers in Selling*. New York: HarperCollins, 1994.

Lewis, Adele Beatrice. *Better Resumes for Sales and Marketing Personnel*. Hauppauge, NY: Barron's Educational Series, 1996.

Lewis, Herschell G. and Robert D. Lewis. *Selling on the Net: The Complete Guide*. Lincolnwood, IL: NTC Business Books, 1997.

Lipow, Valerie. *Retailing Career Starter*. Learning Express, 1998.

Lytle, Chris. *The Accidental Salesperson: How to Take Control of Your Sales Career and Earn the Respect and Income You Deserve*. New York: Amacom, 2000.

Maltz, Maxwell. *Zero-Resistance Selling*. Englewood, NJ: Prentice-Hall, 1998.

Pancero, Jim. *Leading Your Sales Team*. Chicago: The Dartnell Corporation, 1995.

Parinello, Anthony. *Complete Idiot's Guide to Dynamic Selling*. Alpha Books, 1998.

Sheppard, Shaun. *Clinch the Deal: Selling the Professional Way*. Surrey, UK: Elliot Right Way Books, 2001.

The Editors of VGM Career Books. *Resumes for Sales and Marketing Careers*. Lincolnwood, IL: VGM Career Books, 1998.

Sixty Most Memorable Sales: From "Selling Power" Readers. Personal Selling Power, 2000.

Williams, Jane. *Insider's Guide to the World of Pharmaceutical Sales*. Principle Publications, 2000.

REPRESENTATIVE PROFESSIONAL ASSOCIATIONS

The following professional associations may be good sources of information about employment opportunities, available training, or more general facts about various industries. Please note that much of this list is provided courtesy of the National Electrical Manufacturers Representatives Association.

Agricultural & Industrial Manufacturers Representatives Association
5818 Reeds Road
Mission, KS 66202

Aircraft Electronics Association
P.O. Box 1981
Independence, MO 64055

American Hardware Manufacturers Association
801 Plaza Drive
Schaumburg, IL 60194

American Lighting Association
Box 580168
Dallas, TX 75258-0168

American Society of Refrigeration & Air Conditioning
    Engineers
217 International Circle
Hunt Valley, MD 21030

Association of Industry Manufacturers Representatives
222 Merchandise Mart Plaza, #1360
Chicago, IL 60654

Association of Sales and Marketing Companies
2100 Reston Parkway, Suite 400
Reston, VA 22091-1208

Association of Visual Merchandise Representatives
17610 Midway Road, Suite 133-340
Dallas, TX 75252

Automotive Service Industry Association
1460 E-W Highway, Suite 300
Bethesda, MD 20814-3415

Canadian Electrical Manufacturers Representatives Association
c/o Electro-Federation
10 Carlson Court, Suite 210
Etobicoke, ON M9W 6L2
Canada

Canadian Institute of Plumbing and Heating
295 The West Mall
Toronto, ON M9C 4Z4
Canada

Canadian Office Products Association
4920 de Maisonneuve, Suite 305
Westmount, Quebec H3Z 1N1
Canada

Canadian Professional Sales Association
145 Wellington Street West, Suite 610
Toronto, ON M5J 1H8
Canada

Communication Marketing Association
2111 Greenspring Drive
Timonium, MD 21093

Customer Relationship Management Association
    (CRMA) Canada
411 Richmond Street East
Toronto, ON M5A 3S5
Canada

Electrical Equipment Representatives Association
406 West Thirty-fourth Street, Suite 628
Kansas City, MO 64111-2736

Electrical Generating Systems Association
10251 D West Sample Road
Coral Spring, FL 33065

Electronics Representatives Association
20 East Huron Street
Chicago, IL 60611

Health Industry Representatives Association
5818 Reeds Road
Mission, KS 66202

Independent Professional Representatives Association
P.O. Box 4146
Deerfield Beach, FL 33442

Industrial Representatives Association
21010 Ridge Road
Rocky River, OH 44116

International Association of Plastics Distributors
4707 College Boulevard, Suite 300
McLean, VA 22012

International Manufacturers Representatives Association
P.O. Box 702-678
Tulsa, OK 74170

Manufacturers Agents Association of North America
15 Toronto Street
Toronto, ON M5C 2R1
Canada

Manufacturers Representatives Educational Research
    Foundation (MRERF)
P.O. Box 247
Geneva, IL 60611-4267

Mechanical Equipment Manufacturers Representatives
P.O. Box 315
Monkton, MD 21111

National Association of Lighting Representatives
P.O. Box 214
Sea Girt, NJ 08750

National Electrical Manufacturers Representatives Association
660 White Plains Road, Suite 600
Tarrytown, NY 10591

National Groundwater Association
1901 Embarcadero Road, Suite 106
Palo Alto, CA 94303

National Screw Machine Products Association
6700 West Snowville Road
Brecksville, OH 44141

National Tooling and Machining Association
9300 Livingston Road
Fort Washington, MD 20744

North American Industrial Representatives Association
175 North Harbor Drive, Suite 1205
Chicago, IL 60601

Office Products Representatives Alliance
301 North Fairfax Street
Alexandria, VA 22314

Power-Motion Tech Representatives Association
330 South Wells Street, Suite 1422
Chicago, IL 60606

Power Transmission Representatives Association
5818 Reeds Road
Mission, KS 66202

Safety Equipment Manufacturers Agents Association
175 North Harbor Drive, Suite 1205
Chicago, IL 60601

Sales Association of the Chemical Industry
66 Morris Avenue, Suite 2A
Springfield, NJ 07081

Specialty Equipment Market Association
P.O. Box 4910
Diamond Bar, CA 91765

United Association of Manufacturers Representatives
P.O. Box 986
Dana Point, CA 92629

COLLEGES OFFERING SALES-RELATED PROGRAMS

U.S. COLLEGES

Following is a list of some of the U.S. colleges and universities offering programs in sales, marketing, or related areas.

Some of these institutions offer degree or certificate programs in sales, while others include sales courses within a marketing program or other business program, or cover sale-related concepts in other courses. In addition, please note that this is not an all-inclusive list, but rather a representative one.

For names and addresses of other schools offering such programs, contact the appropriate state higher education agency for information, and then request a catalog or other information directly from the college or university in question. Almost all schools also maintain websites where further information may be obtained.

If you are unsure about majoring in marketing or a sales-related area, keep in mind that two-year colleges can be a great place to start. Contact the office of admissions at any local community college to find out more.

Abilene Christian University
Abilene, TX 79699

Adams State College
Alamosa, CO 81102

Adelphi University
Garden City, NY 11530

University of Akron
Akron, OH 44325

University of Alabama
Tuscaloosa, AL 35487

Alfred University
Alfred, NY 14802

American University
Washington, D.C. 20016

Appalachian State University
Boone, NC 28608

University of Arizona
Tucson, AZ 85721

Arizona State University
Tempe, AZ 85287

University of Arkansas
Fayetteville, AR 72701

Auburn University at Montgomery
Montgomery, AL 36142

Austin Peay State University
Clarksville, TN 37044

Ball State University
Muncie, IN 47306

Baylor University
Waco, TX 76798

Boise State University
Boise, ID 83725

Boston College
Chestnut Hill, MA 02467

Brigham Young University
Provo, UT 84602

University at Buffalo, State University of New York
Buffalo, NY 14620

University of California, Los Angeles
Los Angeles, CA 90095

California State University, San Marcos
San Marcos, CA 92096

Central Connecticut State University
New Britain, CT 06050

University of Central Florida
Orlando, FL 32816

Central Michigan University
Mount Pleasant, MI 48859

Central State University
Wilberforce, OH 45384

Charleston Southern University
Charleston, SC 29423

University of Cincinnati
Cincinnati, OH 45221

Clark University
Worcester, MA 01610

Clemson University
Clemson, SC 29634

Cleveland State University
Cleveland, OH 44115

University of Colorado at Boulder
Boulder, CO 80309

Colorado State University
Fort Collins, CO 80907

Concord College
Athens, WV 24712

University of Connecticut
Storrs, CT 06269

Creighton University
Omaha, NE 68178

University of Dayton
Dayton, OH 45469

University of Delaware
Newark, DE 19716

DePaul University
Chicago, IL 60604

Drake University
Des Moines, IA 50311

Duke University
Durham, NC 27708

East Carolina University
Greenville, NC 27858

East Tennessee State University
Johnson City, TN 37614

Eastern Michigan University
Ypsilanti, MI 48197

Elon College
Elon, NC 27244

Fairfield University
Fairfield, CT 06430

University of Florida
Gainesville, FL 32611

Florida State University
Tallahassee, FL 32306

Frostburg State University
Frostburg, MD 21532

George Mason University
Fairfax, VA 22030

University of Georgia
Athens, GA 30602

Georgia Southern University
Statesboro, GA 30460

Grambling State University
Grambling, LA 71245

University of Hawaii at Hilo
Hilo, HI 96720

Hofstra University
Hempstead, NY 11549

University of Houston
Houston, TX 77004

Idaho State University
Pocatello, ID 83209

Illinois State University
Normal, IL 61790

Indiana University
South Bend, IN 46634

University of Iowa
Iowa City, IA 52242

Iowa State University
Ames, IA 50011

Jacksonville University
Jacksonville, FL 32211

James Madison University
Harrisonburg, VA 22807

University of Kansas
Lawrence, KS 66045

Kansas State University
Manhattan, KS 66506

Kent State University
Kent, OH 44242

University of Kentucky
Lexington, KY 40506

Kutztown University
Kutztown, PA 19530

Longwood College
Farmville, VA 23909

Louisiana State University
Baton Rouge, LA 70803

University of Louisville
Louisville, KY 40292

Luther College
Decorah, IA 52101

Madonna University
Livonia, MI 48150

University of Maine
Augusta, ME 04330

Marist College
Poughkeepsie, NY 12601

Marquette University
Milwaukee, WI 53201

Marshall University
Huntington, WV 25755

University of Maryland
College Park, MD 20742

University of Massachusetts-Amherst
Amherst, MA 01003

University of Memphis
Memphis, TN 38152

Mesa State College
Grand Junction, CO 81502

University of Michigan
Ann Arbor, MI 48109

Michigan State University
East Lansing, MI 48824

Middle Tennessee State University
Murfreesboro, TN 37132

University of Minnesota
Duluth, MN 55812

University of Mississippi
University, MS 38677

Mississippi State University
Mississippi State, MS 39762

University of Missouri–Columbia
Columbia, MO 65211

University of Montana
Missoula, MT 59812

Montclair State University
Upper Montclair, NJ 07043

Murray State University
Murray, KY 42071

University of Nebraska–Lincoln
Lincoln, NE 68588

University of Nevada–Reno
Reno, NV 89557

University of New Mexico
Albuquerque, NM 87131

New Mexico State University
Las Cruces, NM 88003

Niagara University
Niagara University, NY 14109

University of North Carolina at Chapel Hill
Chapel Hill, NC 27599

North Carolina State University
Raleigh, NC 27695

University of North Dakota
Grand Forks, ND 58202

Northeastern University
Boston, MA 02115

Northern Arizona University
Flagstaff, AZ 86011

Northern Illinois University
De Kalb, IL 60115

University of Northern Iowa
Cedar Falls, IA 50614

Ohio University
Athens, OH 45701

Ohio State University
Columbus, OH 43210

University of Oklahoma
Norman, OK 73019

Oklahoma State University
Stillwater, OK 74078

Old Dominion University
Norfolk, VA 23529

Oregon State University
Corvallis, OR 97331

Pace University
New York, NY 10038

Pennsylvania State University
University Park, PA 16802

Pepperdine University
Malibu, CA 90263

University of Phoenix
Phoenix, AZ 85072

University of Pittsburgh
Pittsburgh, PA 15260

Purdue University
West Lafayette, IN 47907

Quinnipiac College
Hamden, CT 06518

University of Rhode Island
Kingston, RI 02881

Robert Morris College
Moon Township, PA 15108

Rollins College
Winter Park, FL 32789

Rutgers University–Camden
Camden, NJ 08102

St. Bonaventure University
St. Bonaventure, NY 14778

St. John's University
Jamaica, NY 11439

Sam Houston State University
Huntsville, TX 77341

San Diego State University
San Diego, CA 92182

San Francisco State University
San Francisco, CA 94132

Seton Hall University
South Orange, NJ 07079

Shenandoah University
Winchester, VA 22601

University of South Carolina
Columbia, SC 29208

Southern Connecticut State University
New Haven, CT 06515

Southern Methodist University
Dallas, TX 75275

The University of Southern Mississippi
Hattiesburg, MS 39406

Southwest Missouri State University
Springfield, MO 65802

State University of New York at Stony Brook
Stony Brook, NY 11794

Stonehill College
Easton, MA 02357

Temple University
Philadelphia, PA 19122

University of Tennessee
Knoxville, TN 37996

University of Texas
Austin, TX 78712

University of Toledo
Toledo, OH 43606

Troy State University
Troy, AL 36082

Tulane University
New Orleans, LA 70118

Utah State University
Logan, UT 84322

Valdosta State University
Valdosta, GA 31698

University of Vermont
Burlington, VT 05405

Villanova University
Villanova, PA 19085

University of Virginia
Charlottesville, VA 22903

Virginia Polytechnic Institute and State University (Virginia Tech)
Blacksburg, VA 24061

Wake Forest University
Winston-Salem, NC 27109

University of Washington
Seattle, WA 98195

Wayne State University
Detroit, MI 48202

West Virginia University
Morgantown, WV 26506

Western Carolina University
Cullowhee, NC 28723

Wichita State University
Wichita, KS 67260

University of Wisconsin–Madison
Madison, WI 53706

University of Wyoming
Laramie, WY 82071

Youngstown State University
Youngstown, OH 44555

CANADIAN COLLEGES

Many of Canada's colleges and universities offer programs in sales or in related areas. Following is a list of selected institutions offering such programs. Other colleges also may offer programs of interest, or if not full-scale programs, individual courses in sales principles or related subjects.

For more details, contact schools in your area or in other geographic regions you find of interest. Request a catalog along with details on courses in sales, marketing, or business management.

Alberta College
10050 MacDonald Drive
Edmonton, AB T5J 2B7

Algonquin College
1385 Woodroffe Avenue
Nepean, ON K2G 1V8

British Columbia Institute of Technology
3700 Willingdon Avenue
Burnaby, BC V5G 3H2

George Brown College
P.O. Box 1015, Station B
Toronto, ON M5T 2T9

Holland College
Charlottestown, PE C1A 4Z1

Humber College
205 Humber College Boulevard
Toronto, ON M9W 5L7

Langara College
100 West Forty-ninth Avenue
Vancouver, BC V5Y 2Z6

Loyalist College
P.O. Box 4200
Wallbridge-Loyalist Road
Belleville, ON K8N 5B9

Niagra College of Applied Arts and Technology
P.O. Box 1005
Welland, ON L3B 5S2

Nova Scotia Community College
P.O. Box 550
Truro, NS B2N 5E3

Red River College
2055 Notre Dame Avenue
Winnipeg, MB R3H 0J9

Sault College of Applied Arts and Technology
443 Northern Avenue
Sault St. Marie, ON P6A 5L3

Southern Alberta Institute of Technology
1301 Sixteenth Avenue NW
Calgary, AL T2M 0L4

University College of the Fraser Valley
Abbotsford, BC V2S 7M9

GLOSSARY

accounts payable. An accounting entry noting an amount owed by a business to a creditor (may also refer to the department or personnel handling such matters).

accounts receivable. An accounting entry noting an amount due to a business for products sold on credit (may also refer to the department or personnel handling such matters).

advertising allowance. Financial support provided by a manufacturer to a retailer for advertising the manufacturer's products.

allowance. A discount, temporary reduction in price, or other incentive that a manufacturer offers to a retailer.

ANSI. An acronym for American National Standards Institute, this is a clearinghouse for U.S. electronic data standards in the United States, which are becoming increasingly important in electronic commerce.

assets. Everything that a business owns, such as cash, merchandise, equipment, investments, or real estate.

banded pack. Packaging in which products are banded together for sale at a reduced price.

bar code.   A pattern of encoded information made up of spaces and bars that can be read by a scanner or bar code reader.

bench marking.   The practice of measuring performance against that of competitors or preestablished standards for comparison purposes.

bill of lading.   A business document that indicates goods received will be shipped to a designated destination.

bonus goods.   Products given to a retailer by a manufacturer as a bonus for volume purchases.

brand development index.   A method of calculating how much of a given brand is consumed in a specific time period.

brand image.   The overall impressions held by consumers about a given brand.

carrier.   A commercial enterprise responsible for transporting a shipment.

category management.   The practice of regarding distinct product categories as individual business units for strategic purposes.

CFR.   An acronym for Collaborative Forecasting and Replenishment, a practice in which companies work together to forecast product demand and plan for the necessary product delivery.

channel.   The path that takes products from manufacturers to consumers.

consignment sales.   Sales in which payment is made to a supplier only for those products that are sold on the supplier's behalf by a retailer, with unsold products returned to the supplier.

corporation. An entity legally entitled to carry on business activity or related functions.

customer relations. Relationships between sales personnel or other company staff and customers.

E-commerce. Also know as E-business, the practice of using the Internet or related forms of electronic communication.

electronic funds transfer. Also known as EFT, the processing of payments by electronic means.

F.O.B. An abbreviation for "free on board," normally referring to the point to which shipment costs will be paid by the manufacturer or seller, with shipping costs beyond that point assumed by the purchaser.

forecasting. The practice of predicting sales in advance of actual sales transactions.

full disclosure. Full and detailed information provided by manufacturers about features of their products.

gross margin. Business profit as calculated before operating expenses are deducted.

guaranteed sales. A guarantee by a supplier that it will take back goods that it provides to a retailer if the retailer is unable to sell them.

impulse purchase. A purchase in which the buyer has acted spontaneously without previously planning to make the purchase.

incentive. A reward provided to sales personnel or others for achieving or exceeding specified performance levels.

invoice.   A bill for goods or services.

island display.   A product display in a store environment that may be viewed from all sides.

key account.   A primary or especially important customer.

logistics.   The area of business dealing with transporting, storing, and distributing goods.

logo.   A stylized, graphic, or artistic representation of a company name.

market.   The demand for goods or services.

market share.   The proportion of sales that a company, or a given product, maintains out of overall sales for similar companies or products.

picking.   The selection of a stockroom or warehouse, usually for shipment.

refund.   Funds that are returned to a customer when goods are returned, in some cases coming in the form of a credit.

retail sales.   Sales of goods or services to the consumer.

return on investment (ROI).   The amount of profit in a business activity compared to the amount of resources needed to generate that profit.

RFP.   An acronym for Request for Proposal, which is a document in which potential suppliers of a product or service are invited to describe how they would meet the need established in the RFP.

shrinkage. Losses sustained from theft or other problems causing lost inventory.

TQM. An acronym for Total Quality Management, a management approach emphasizing continuous improvement of business.

warranty. A written document that guarantees the seller (or manufacturer) assumes responsibility for a product's effectiveness or quality.